Palos Verdes Peninsula

Time and the Terraced Land

Ron Howard

Palos Verdes Peninsula

Time and the Terraced Land

by Augusta Fink

Western Tanager Press

1987

Western Tanager Press
1111 Pacific Ave.
Santa Cruz, CA 95060
Jacket Design by Lynn Piquett.
Originally published in 1966 as *Time and the Terraced Land* by Howell-
North Books.
Library of Congress Catalog Card No. 66-18957
ISBN 0–934136–37–8

ACKNOWLEDGMENTS

TO THE MANY people who helped in the preparation of this book, I am deeply grateful.

For their invaluable contributions to my original research, I am especially indebted to the following individuals: the late Dr. Richard H. Jahns, Professor of Geology and Dean, School of Earth Sciences, Stanford University, for providing the material on the geological evolution of the Peninsula; the late Bernice Johnston for personal consultation on the Gabrielino Indians and for editing that chapter of the book; and the late John G. Nordin, of Great Lakes Carbon Corporation, for giving unstintingly of his time to make important sources available. Special thanks are also due the late Ellen Barrett, of the Los Angeles City Library, for supplying the genealogical data on the Sepúlveda family.

Enough appreciation cannot be expressed to Anna Marie and Everett Gordon Hager, who shared their superb, personal library on Harbor history, assisted in readying the first edition of the book for publication, and gave their continuing guidance and support.

For their consideration in connection with my original research, I am also indebted to Jane Loughrin, Elin Vanderlip, Harry Phillips, Jr., Mrs. S.Y. Warner, Mrs. George Gibbs, Mrs. Donald Armstrong, Mrs. Paul Saffo, Harry Benedict, Howard Towle, Walter Davis, William Emerson, William Campeau, Mrs. Weare Pearson II, Mrs. Charles Houghton, and Remi Nadeau.

Credits for the pictures are given throughout the book, but I wish to express special appreciation for the photographs taken by William Webb and for the original art work in the maps made by Jack Moffett. For assistance in the selection of the historical photographs, I am grateful to the staffs of the Palos Verdes Library, the Seaver Center for Western History Research, and the Henry Huntington Library.

I am also profoundly indebted to Mrs. Marguerite C. Douglas for permission to reproduce the oil painting by Raymond E. Wallace in the cover design and to Mr. Wallace for his gracious assistance.

Finally, my deepest gratitude goes to Dr. Lois Roberts, who gave most generously of her time and expertise in researching the materials necessary for the updating of the book.

Augusta Fink
Carmel
November, 1986

The old whaling station at Portuguese Bend, as it actually appeared in 1885. *(Painting by Raymond E. Wallace, Courtesy John G. Nordin)*

Contents

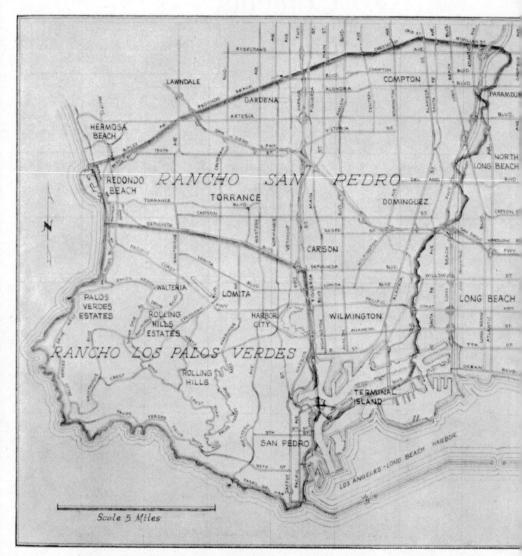

Extent of original grant of the Rancho San Pedro and the Rancho de los Palos Verdes. *(Jack Moffett)*

Preface

THIS IS THE STORY of one of California's oldest ranchos. It is also the story of a unique land formation. In a sense, the two stories are inextricably interwoven, for the shape of the land determined its development and molded the lives of the people who dwelt upon it.

The plot begins, millions of years ago, with the evolution of the majestic land mass which is now called the Palos Verdes Peninsula. Moving forward through the ages, the cast of characters includes gentle Indian folk, swashbuckling Spanish soldiers, pirates and pioneers, dashing dons and fervent friars, and finally enterprising Yankees and modern entrepreneurs. The setting is the dramatic history of California as a whole. The protagonist is the Rancho de los Palos Verdes.

In the beginning, before this beautiful rancho had an identity of its own, it was part of California's first private land concession. Three years after the founding of Los Angeles, a Spanish soldier received, in recognition of his faithful service to the crown, a princely domain covering 75,000 acres. The year was 1784. The soldier was Juan José Domínguez. The land grant was named Rancho San Pedro.

This munificent land grant encompassed the present-day communities of Redondo Beach, Torrance, Compton, Gardena, Lomita, Harbor City, Dominguez, Carson, Wilmington, the western portion of Long

Beach and the entire Palos Verdes Peninsula, including San Pedro.

Less than three decades later, well over a third of this land was in the possession of a courageous young boy named José Dolores Sepúlveda. The Rancho de los Palos Verdes had come into being.

In terms of today's landmarks, it was bounded on the north by Sepulveda Boulevard, on the east by Figueroa Street and the Los Angeles Harbor, and on the south and west by the Pacific Ocean. Within these boundaries are not only the four Peninsula cities of Palos Verdes Estates, Rancho Palos Verdes, Rolling Hills, and Rolling Hills Estates, but also Lomita, Walteria, and Harbor City, as well as San Pedro, which is a part of the City of Los Angeles.

Literally translated, Palos Verdes means green sticks; freely translated, green trees. According to W. W. Robinson, one of the best historians of the Los Angeles area, the name originated with the "Cañada de Palos Verdes." The canyon was part of a lovely, little valley located between what are now the Harbor Freeway and Figueroa Street, just south of Sepulveda Boulevard. Cool, green, and lush with water, willow trees, and grass, this valley was apparently a favorite stopping place for early travelers along the long, dusty trail to San Pedro Harbor, as it shows on old maps of the area.

The story of the "Rancho of the Green Trees" is as captivating as its spectacular landscape. It is told in response to a multitude of requests from those who have the good fortune to live within its boundaries. Sensitive to the quiet, yet powerful, influence of the past upon the present, they are aware that an appreciation of the history of their homeland will add to their enjoyment of it. Proud of their heritage, they want to share its story with relatives and friends in distant places.

For those who can visit the Palos Verdes Peninsula only briefly, but are captured by its spellbinding beauty, it is hoped that this book will enhance the experience and provide a lasting memento. Finally, there is the wish that the story of the Rancho de los Palos Verdes will fill in one more crevice in the magnificent panorama of California history and contribute to the proposition that history should be a glorious entertainment.

Introduction

ACROSS THE BROAD SWATH of the Los Angeles Basin, southwest of the San Gabriel Mountains, a proud prow of land thrusts out to sea. The fascinating story of how this shape of beauty came to be could reach back over a hundred million years, when the interplay of uplift, erosion, and deposition that was to give the Palos Verdes Peninsula its unique physiography may already have begun. The farther back in geologic time one goes, the more difficult it becomes to piece together what actually happened. However, starting about fifteen million years ago, it is known that the whole region of which the Peninsula is a part was then submerged under the Pacific Ocean.

Also, at that time, a great rim of mountains had risen to form a bastion around a huge arm of the sea off today's coastline. This enormous mountain chain is now partially represented by the Santa Ana, the San Gabriel, and the Santa Monica Mountains, while its remnants comprise the Channel Islands. As the rim of mountains was progressively uplifted, processes of erosion and stream transportation slowly contributed vast quantities of sedimentary debris to the adjacent marine basin, which occupied an area of forty to seventy miles across.

Although it has not been possible to assign specific time intervals to the emergence of the Peninsula, it is known that it coincided, at least in part, with the Ice Age, when sea levels fluctuated throughout the world. A couple of million years ago, it was an island, separated from the upper Los Angeles Basin by the sea. It is believed that it emerged more than once. The uplift was progressive but the rate varied considerably, at times taking place very slowly and at others relatively rapidly. During the slow stages of the uplift, when the sea level remained fairly constant in relation to the land, the ocean cut broad steps or terraces into the rocks. Thus were formed the terraces which are such a distinctive feature of the Peninsula's physiography.

Thirteen main wave-cut terraces have been formally identified, but actually there are hundreds, of which about twenty-five are readily observable. Terrace surfaces are present on all sides of the Peninsula but they are best developed on the seaward side, which was exposed to the strongest cutting force of the waves. A terrace is, of course, a landform that is modified with time, both through deposition from above and through erosion in the form of gullies and canyons. Each successive terrace has been incised by lines of drainage, including deep canyons in the highest ones, and each has been eaten into by the sea during the period when the next lower terrace was being cut. The lower and intermediate terraces are generally better preserved than the highest ones, because they have not been exposed to erosion for as long a time.

Before the end of the last glacial period, sedimentary deposition from the mountains to the north, comprising a vast accumulation of rock, gravel, and silt, filled the gap that had separated the Peninsula from the mainland. At one time this area was a veritable jungle of trees, laced by hidden swamps and lakes. Although the "forest" has disappeared, a slight indication of what the terrain was like may be seen around old Lake Machado, now called Harbor Lake, at the intersection of Palos Verdes Drive North and Gaffey and Anaheim Streets.

Today, the Peninsula rises majestically from the flat floor of the Los Angeles Basin, stretching nine miles by five miles, and covering approximately twenty-two thousand acres. Situated between two bays, the profile of the Peninsula is visible forty miles to the southwest and as far north as Point Mugu, about forty-five miles. The high ridge of the Palos Verdes Hills reaches an altitude of 1480 feet at the top of San Pedro Hill and forms one of the most prominent landmarks along the California coast.

Two and a half miles from the summit, the southeastern extremity of the ridge forms Point Fermin. Then, for eighteen miles around the shoreline of the Peninsula, steep, rocky cliffs rise from fifty to three hundred feet above the sea. Between these and the crest of the ridge is the succession of sweeping terraces for which the Peninsula is renowned around the world. At several points, the terraces are incised by steep-walled canyons. One of these, Malaga Canyon, cuts through the north slopes of the Palos Verdes Hills, then swings west to empty at Malaga Cove, the northwestern extremity of the Peninsula.

Crossing Malaga Canyon, Palos Verdes Drive West comes to the charming hill-town of Palos Verdes Estates. For many people, this delightful community is reminiscent of the French Riviera or the Isle of Capri. Ethel Barrymore, who once lived here, wrote in her book, "Memories"—"It was entirely different from any other place in Southern California where I had been. A place of magical beauty."

In the center of the Palos Verdes Plaza, a striking marble fountain, which is an exact replica of the famed La Fontana del Nettuno in Bologna, Italy, adds to the wonderful old world atmosphere. Two-thirds the size of the original, it once stood for a hundred years in the courtyard of an old Italian villa north of Venice. A gift to the community by its founders, it was dismantled and brought to Palos Verdes in 1930, where the delicate work of reassembling it was engineered by G. Brooks Snelgrove. Surmounted by a statue of Neptune and surrounded by seahorses, cupids, and mermaids, the fountain has since suffered many vicissitudes at the hands of vandals. Also, in 1968, the statue deteriorated and finally collapsed, due to corrosion of the steel rods in its legs. Replaced by a second replica, carved in Italy, the powerful figure once again graces the city's stunning landmark.

Continuing on Palos Verdes Drive West, as it curves out along the coastline, spectacular seascapes burst into view. Here the ocean may be a deep cobalt blue, with splashes of amethyst and jade, or a gleaming stretch of polished pewter, spotlighted by broad areas of sparkling silver. Looking down into Bluff Cove, one sees the backs of huge combers as they explode in high plumes of spray. To the north, across the sweep of Santa Monica Bay, is the multilayered silhouette of the Santa Monica Mountains, and on the far horizon are the blunt outlines of the Channel Islands.

A few miles farther on, the shoreline juts out to form the massive headland of Palos Verdes, or Rocky Point. From here, practically perpendicular cliffs circle the half-moon of Lunada Bay to Resort Point. This is a good place to observe the profile of terraces sweeping up from the shore. High on their windswept bluffs, like eagle eyries, a myriad of houses crouch. And through their tawny curves, Agua Amarga Canyon slices out to sea. Far below, at the base of Rocky Point, fragments of the Greek freighter, *Dominator,* may be seen at low tide, mute testimony to the treacherous reefs that surround the bay.

Now, as the coastline of the Peninsula curves to the south, the western end of Catalina Island looms on the horizon. Along this stretch of scalloped shoreline, honeycombed with caves created by centuries of pounding surf, are several interesting landmarks. The first of these is Point Vicente, named in the 1790s by Captain George Vancouver for his good friend Friar Vicente of the Mission Buenaventura. Here, since 1926, the Point Vicente Lighthouse has stood guard over the safety of seacraft. Today, adjacent to the lighthouse, the Point Vicente Interpretive Center offers the visitor fascinating insights into the history and geology of the Peninsula, as well as the opportunity to glimpse gray whales during their annual migration. Situated on nineteen acres of parkland, the museum includes scientific and historical exhibits, information about the Pacific gray whale, and a display of Indian artifacts.

Next in view is Long Point, once the site of a renowned 108-acre aquatic park called Marineland. Brainchild of a New York stockbroker, it first opened its doors in August, 1954, and over the ensuing thirty-three years provided a unique encounter with the wonders of the world's oceans for millions of visitors. Here one could observe killer whales, dolphins, walruses, sea lions, and sharks, all at close range. Thirty-four tanks offered an intimate view of rare and exotic marine life, while experienced swimmers could also enjoy a swim-through aquarium, termed the "Baja Reef," because it duplicated the underwater community off Baja California. The Marineland was also noted for its scientific research and included a facility for the life-saving treatment of ailing marine animals and birds. In January, 1987, the aquatic park was acquired by the publishing firm, Harcourt Brace Jovanovich, owners of Sea World parks in San Diego, California, and Orlando, Florida. A month later, the new owners determined that continuing operation of the Palos Verdes Peninsula facility would not be cost-effective and announced its permanent closure. Marine inhabitants were transported to other Sea World parks, and negotiations were initiated with the city of Rancho Palos Verdes regarding the use to be made of the scenic stretch of coastland.

Proceeding along Palos Verdes Drive South, one approaches Abalone Cove, a rendezvous of Yankee smugglers in bygone years. From here the full length of Catalina Island rims the horizon, and above the highway, nestled in the hills, is the Wayfarer's Chapel—a soaring edifice of redwood, glass, and stone. Designed by Lloyd Wright, well-known architect and son of Frank Lloyd Wright, it was dedicated in 1951 as a memorial to Emanuel Swedenborg. The idea for this unique place of worship originated with Elizabeth Schellenberg, daughter of a Swedenborgian minister and early resident of Palos Verdes, as an expression of her faith in harmony with the beauty of the Peninsula. Erected on land donated by Mrs. Frank Vanderlip, Sr. and built with the help of her son, Kelvin Vanderlip, the "glass church," as it is colloquially called, has inspired people of all faiths by its simple services and the vast panorama of sea and sky visible through its luminous walls.

Beyond Abalone Cove is historic Portuguese Bend, named after the two Portuguese whaling companies which operated here in the middle of the nineteenth century. It was in this area that tragedy struck, with the landslide that began in the summer of 1956, destroying over one hundred homes. Residents had practically no warning.

First a water line ruptured, and service crews discovered an offset of several inches in the pipeline. Then, within a matter of days, houses started to shift. When told to evacuate their homes, residents couldn't believe it. Soon gaping crevices opened up in living areas and sections of ceilings fell. Many residents had to be rescued in the middle of the night. Those who were determined to stay lost everything.

The property involved, about 270 acres, covers a portion of an ancient landslide, which had been known to geologists for many years. In the early 1950s, the Los Angeles County Road Department began a construction project to extend Crenshaw Boulevard across the Palos Verdes Hills to Palos Verdes Drive South. Construction work crossed the slide mass, then dormant. Experts believe that the excavation of thousands of yards of rock and movement of the material to a critical location below the landslide escarpment caused the reactivation of the ground movement.

Though the rate of movement has slowed from an initial four inches a day to less than one inch, it has been continuous for the past thirty years, twisting and contorting the road that traverses it. A portion of the thoroughfare had to be relocated twice, and it has cost the City of Rancho Palos Verdes, within which the slide area lies, as much as $200,000 annually to keep the .8-mile stretch of roadway open through the landslide.

Since the mid-1970s, two additional landslides have been in progress immediately adjacent to the Portuguese Bend slide. One is in the area of Abalone Cove, where the Wayfarer's Chapel has sustained damage and more than a hundred homes have been threatened; the other lies to the east in the Klondike Canyon region. The mechanics which triggered the ground movement—the driving force derived from faulting within the landslide and the accumulation of ground water due to heavy rainfall—are believed to be similar in some respects to those evinced in the Portuguese Bend area. Two Geologic Hazard Abatement Districts have been formed to finance continued geologic investigation of the slides and installation of mine dewatering wells. These measures appear to have reduced lateral movement.

Meanwhile, the City of Rancho Palos Verdes is planning a $2,000,000 project to curb the creeping Portuguese Bend landslide by moving 400,000 cubic yards of earth towards the ocean to act as a resisting force. It has also entered into a joint effort with the City of Rolling Hills, its neighbor in the hills to the north, to investigate causes of a fourth landslide, termed the "Flying Triangle," which began in 1980 and has crossed to the eastern side of Klondike Canyon.

Despite the vicissitudes which have defaced a stretch of the Peninsula's southern flank, the shape of beauty endures, continuing to beguile the senses with its stunning landscapes. Past Portuguese Bend the road winds through rolling meadows to where it divides to mount the skyline of the Palos Verdes Hills. Here, as both sea and land seem to drop away, there is a magnificent panoramic view of the Pacific. A vast expanse of shining sea stretches to the far horizon, with Santa Catalina sculptured along its rim and San Clemente Island to the south. Rarely is the channel without a steady stream of traffic: lumber ships, coastal liners, fishing boats, and pleasure craft, approaching or leaving Los Angeles Harbor.

After the first big loop in the road, it is possible to turn left again and climb to the top of San Pedro Hill. From here the neck of the Peninsula is visible, with the beach cities circling Santa Monica Bay to the left, and Los Angeles Harbor, Long Beach, and the distant Laguna Hills on the right. Across the broad plain of the Los Angeles Basin, looms the massive San Gabriel Range, with ten-thousand-foot Mount San Antonio (Mt. Baldy) silhouetted against the sky, fifty-five miles away. This is indeed one of the most breathtaking of all the many marvelous scenic sights on the Peninsula.

Descending from the crest of the ridge, one drops down the northeastern slopes of the hills, alongside Georgeff Canyon, to the reservoir. From here Palos Verdes Drive North circles the north side of the Peninsula. To the right, the drive takes one to old Machado Lake, where nearby, the populous Indian village of Suangna once stood for hundreds of years. In the nineteenth century, when Juan Sepúlveda, one of the original owners of the Rancho de los Palos Verdes, built his home high on a hill overlooking the lake, the village was still there.

To the left of the reservoir, the drive traverses green and golden hills, dotted with clusters of pine and eucalyptus and fringed by a long line of lacy-leafed pepper trees. Here broad country vistas surround rambling ranch houses, and sleek horses graze inside white rail fences. Far below, one catches occasional glimpses of the Los Angeles Basin and the distant mountains beyond it. At Crenshaw Boulevard, one of the main thoroughfares off the Peninsula, the drive crosses another broad canyon cutting through the north slopes of the hills.

Named Agua Negra, because of the adobe-blackened water which washed through its walls, this canyon harbors the remnants of several old quarries. These were developed in one of the richest sources of diatomite in California, yielding more than a million tons of it between 1929 and 1958. Diatomite and diatomaceous earth are composed principally of the skeletons of countless microscopic marine plants called diatoms. About ten million years ago, when the Peninsula was submerged under the sea, these organisms accumulated in vast quantities, forming the beds of rock, interlayered with shale and mudstone, which is called diatomite. Because of its great porosity, diatomaceous earth is used as a filter-agent in hundreds of industrial processes. The diatomite mining operation, now long abandoned, played a crucial role in the history of the Peninsula, as in 1953, it prompted the Great Lakes Carbon Corporation to purchase a lion's share of the Peninsula, thus significantly affecting its subsequent development.

Over the years, a multitude of changes have taken place. Perhaps the most startling of these is the present-day "Town Center," located within the City of Rolling Hills Estates. Once its site was a lovely valley occupied by an enormous farm called Rancho El Elastico, a portion of which later became the home of thoroughbred race horses. Today it encompasses an ultra-modern commercial center, including financial institutions, two shopping malls, several department stores, and hundreds of shops.

Still the Peninsula has maintained its distinctive character. Though million-dollar condominiums now cover the Palos Verdes Hills and palatial contemporary residences are intermingled with the old Mediterranean villas and modest family dwellings, privacy and preservation of the beauty of the land continue to have top priority. Acres of parkland have been set aside and held inviolate. Miles of bridle paths thread the hills. Houses are designed and built with an eye to fitting into the landscape. The passion for privacy is most dramatically demonstrated by the City of Rolling Hills, an incorporated city which consists entirely of three square miles of country estates, completely enclosed by white rail fencing and entered only through guarded gates.

Although the Peninsula adjoins the second largest city in America and includes the gigantic Port of Los Angeles within its geographic boundaries, it remains aloof, mantled in an aura of tranquillity. Self-contained and self-sufficient, its communities have adhered to patterns of living that once made all of California a pastoral paradise. Throughout the ages, from the primitive idyll of the Indians through the rancho days to the present, the shape of the land has influenced its development and molded the lives of the people who dwelt upon it. A journey back through time will tell their compelling story.

1

The Quiet People of the Chaparral

EONS BEFORE the white men knew that far away, across the seas and continents, there was a land they someday would call California, a quiet people dwelt here in peace and plenty. Of the earliest of these inhabitants, only the faintest traces remain, but there is evidence that, over a period of tens of thousands of years, several cultures developed, flourished, and disappeared. Some of the most striking of this evidence was uncovered through archeological excavations at a site located on a high bluff overlooking Malaga Cove on the edge of Palos Verdes Estates. Here were found the remnants of four distinct cultures submerged at four separate, well-defined levels. It is entirely within the realm of possibility that the oldest of these cultures dates back fifty thousand years.

Forever buried in the mists of the past is any sure knowledge of how these people came to be here, but it is believed that they migrated from Asia across the Bering Strait, which at one time may have been dry land and over which the Diomedes Islands still form an easy bridge. From Alaska they probably fanned out over the continent, drifting west from the Great Basin until they reached the ramparts of the Sierra Nevada. Probably they crossed these massive mountains through the same passes

11

discovered and traversed so many thousands of years later by Califor-nia's vanguard of fur trappers, gold seekers, and pioneers.

There is an Indian legend in which it is said that when the earth was created it grew ever to the southwestward, and that the people followed. In this ancient myth may be seen a foreshadowing of the current concept of westward tilt. It is hypothesized that at one time there were as many as 150,000 Indians in California, more than in any part of the United States. Thus, California may well have been the most populous area in the country once before—long before history began.

Intensive work has been carried out by archeologists at a dozen sites in the state in an attempt to trace the evolution of prehistoric man in California; one of the most important sites being that at Malaga Cove. Out of this work certain facts have been established. It is known that the most recent emigrants from the Great Basin were of the Shosho-nean family and therefore relatives of the later renowned Hopi Indians. It is estimated that these people began migrating to California about 500 B.C., forming a great wedge tapering from an expanse of six hundred miles along the Nevada border to about one hundred miles along the seacoast of Los Angeles and Orange Counties.

Gradually, over approximately a thousand years, they began to dif-ferentiate into tribes taking on individual characteristics of political and social structure and religious beliefs. By 1200 A.D., these cultural characteristics had crystallized into the forms found by the Spanish ex-plorers, and there existed a distinctive tribe which the Spanish were to call Gabrielinos, after the San Gabriel Mission. This tribe was the last of the Indian cultures to inhabit the Rancho de los Palos Verdes.

These Gabrielinos were a gentle, friendly folk, who lived hardy, prosperous lives as seafarers, fishermen, and traders. The constant presence of the sea and of the islands across the channel, which they called, with such startling intuition, "mountain ranges in the sea," had a strong influence upon them. From the shining stretch of waters sur-rounding them they derived a sense of security and well-being, believ-ing that in the sea the sacred porpoises swam in an eternal circuit guard-ing the safety of the Gabrielino world. They held their tribesmen on the islands in awe, ascribing to them powers of prophecy and learning from them the elements of their deep religious faith.

Happy and carefree, they were well adjusted to their way of life. When it was necessary to work, they were capable of prolonged, directed effort and performed their tasks with competence and ease. When the demands of the day or the season had been fulfilled, they knew how to enjoy the beauty of the land in which they lived. Many hours were undoubtedly spent sporting on the sea in their wonderfully light, swift canoes, gathering shells along the shore, or just basking in the sun. Highly skilled artisans, they seemed to take pleasure in giving beauty as well as utility to the things they made and must have devoted much time to the delicate carvings they fashioned and to weaving the intricate designs of their fine basketry.

A comely people, they were clean, healthy, and free from disease. Although not tall, they were strong, stocky, and muscular. Their skins were a soft, warm brown, even fair in early youth. From the diaries of the Spanish explorers, it is known that the women were handsome, with lovely eyes and features, and a modest aspect to their faces. Proud of their appearance, they kept their thick, black hair glossy with brushes made of Yucca fiber and used the bulb of the plant as an excellent shampoo. The hair was worn in bangs and long, free-flowing tresses over the shoulders. Liberal use was made of cosmetics, red ochre being applied as make-up as well as protection from the ravages of the weather. Diatomaceous earth was used as a white paint.

Men and children usually went about free from clothing, the men occasionally wearing a small deerskin cape around their shoulders. Women, however, always wore aprons, back and front. Both sexes were given to adornment. The women wore flowers in boas and in their hair, and no one of them was without her beads of steatite, whalebone, or shell. If perhaps she possessed a necklace of thick, half-inch clam shells, she had a real status symbol, as these were also used for money. Earrings were worn by both men and women, those of the women being quite elaborate, hung with pendants of whale's tooth and festooned with feathers.

A people of strong family ties, the Gabrielinos lived in closely knit groups. Everybody belonged to a clan, or large family group, with clan membership being established through the father's side of the family. Villages were made up of one or several clans, and the Village Chief was the leader of the dominant clan. Monogamy was the rule for everybody except the Chief, who was permitted to have several wives as he needed their help to gather the large quantities of food and property which his office obligated him to dispense to guests and visiting officials on public occasions.

Individual families lived in circular dwellings, now called wickiups. These were graphically described by the Spaniards as being shaped like half an orange with the skin side up. They were constructed of a willow framework, thatched with tule or grass, and had two openings: a chimney, or smokehole, in the roof and an entrance in the side. Inside there was a dirt floor, with a central fireplace, or pit, which became progressively deeper as ashes were dug out of it. Of course, the house had no furnishings other than beds consisting of mats and robes.

It was an inflexible rule for the family to rise before dawn and perform the daily ritual of bathing before the sun appeared. According to Gabrielino legend, the sun represented the all-seeing eyes of the great god, Chungichnish, and it was best to prepare for the day under the more benign gaze of the gentler god, Wiyot, symbolized by the moon. After breakfast, the activities of the day got underway.

The women tended to their household tasks. It was their job to gather and to prepare many of the staple items of food. They were responsible for harvesting, digging roots and picking fruits. Often they walked miles over brush-covered, rolling hills, painstakingly bending the heads of grasses and annuals over flat, tightly woven baskets and beating the seeds into them with basketwork paddles. And it was not infrequent for one of them to do this with a baby slung over her shoulders in a hammock made of net.

One of the best sources of seed was Chia, a sage-like plant, which has small, gray-brown seeds with a delightful nutty flavor. This was eaten in many forms, and many years later became so popular with the Spanish that, in 1894, it was sold in Los Angeles stores at six to eight dollars a pound. A complicated procedure was followed by the Indian housewife in preparing the seed for her family to eat. It first had to be parched in a basket with hot stones or live coals, then culled, and finally pounded with mortar and pestle into a fine flour. This was sometimes eaten dry in pinches or diluted in a drink, but more often it was mixed with water to make a soupy-like substance resembling gruel, or baked in little cakes. The flour had a high gluten content, was easily digested, and very nutritious. It was said that one teaspoonful of the seed-meal was sufficient to keep an Indian going for twenty-four hours on a forced march.

In addition to meal, almost all the bulbous plants were a source of food, as were cactus fruit and berries. The berries of one shrub, still very prevalent on the Peninsula, were especially popular. The plant, for which the technical name is *Rhus ovata,* is commonly called Sugar Bush. Its berries, when ripened, are covered with a sour-sweet, sticky substance that can be mixed with water to make a most pleasant drink.

From the myriad broken shells uncovered in ancient kitchen middens, or refuse heaps, along the Palos Verdes Coast, the Gabrielinos must have spent many hours gathering shellfish. This could well have been one of their more enjoyable occupations, especially on a warm, clear day with the sea a gleaming stretch of sapphire blue fringed by high plumes of cresting surf. The sand along the rocky shore must have been loaded with clams, as evidenced by the extensive use made of their shells. Apparently abalone was a great favorite too, as enormous quantities of the shells of this delicious fish were transformed into serving dishes by plugging their apertures with asphaltum.

In the long afternoons, when the food-gathering jobs were over for the day, the women probably gathered in what today would be called a "sewing circle." There they performed the never-ending activity of rolling strands of Yucca and Milkweed fiber against their bare thighs to make thread, string, and cordage. This was woven into a fine material which the Spanish said reminded them of linen, and made into nets, mats, aprons, and other articles of clothing. Skeins of the material were used to weave strips of rabbit fur into beautiful, soft robes, as well as to form an incredibly strong and durable rope.

While the women were engaged in their homemaking activities, the men were busy with their own hardy, rugged tasks. To them belonged the work of hunting, fishing, boatbuilding, and trading. They also had the responsibility for running the government and for the elaborate religious ceremonials which were so much a part of community life. Hunting and fishing were highly essential occupations, as a substantial part of the family diet was made up of meat and fish, and dried fish was used as barter for articles from the inland villages.

All kinds of game were found in the hills and along the shore: mule deer, antelope, coyote, badger, jack rabbit, cottontail, and ground squirrel, and many varieties of bird life, including goose, brown pelican, loon, and sea gull. The men sometimes made elaborate preparations for the hunt, stinging their bodies with nettles as a ritual reminder that they possessed the power to bring the project to a successful conclusion. It was also customary for them to refrain from sexual relations before an expedition and not to eat during the hunt.

Hunting the large sea mammals was an exciting, though arduous, and often dangerous activity. The men went after sea lions, dolphins, and sea otters. Bagging one of these huge creatures, with a harpoon made of animal bone fastened to a slender willow rod by a length of cord, was no small feat. Fortunately it was not necessary to capture the great whale, as frequently, after encounters with killer whales, the wounded monsters drifted ashore.

Many hours were devoted to building the twelve to sixteen-foot boats which they used for fishing forays and for commuting to Santa Catalina Island. Patience, hard work, and great skill were required to make these fine craft, fashioned in the renowned Canaliño tradition, with two prows and sometimes wing-boards as well. Wedges made of bone or antler were used to split driftwood logs into planks, which were then buried in wet sand, with fires built above, to render the boards pliable so that they could be bent into place. Then, with implements made of stone, holes were cut for the strong fiber rope lacings which held the boats together. When the planks were put into place and firmly laced, the canoes were thoroughly calked with asphaltum to make them as waterproof as possible. This substance, actually a tar seepage, is very prevalent on the Peninsula, especially between Malaga Cove and Abalone Cove.

Another type of craft which the men built was a canoe-shaped raft, made by lashing together three long bundles of rushes or "tules." These boats, called by the Spanish "balsa," were bulky but not at all clumsy. They accommodated one or two fishermen, and although appearing to be too fragile for anything but a placid lagoon, they were used regularly on the open sea. Great care was taken to beach them in sheltered spots, and to protect them from the rain, in order to prolong their usefulness.

On days when the men were not engaged in hunting, fishing, or boatbuilding, they set out to trade for articles not readily available along the coast. This activity was more strenuous than one might think. The only form of locomotion was on foot, and it was a long, hard hike, over many miles of rough terrain, to trade with a village such as Yangna, the site of present day Los Angeles, or Sibangna, the place where San Gabriel Mission later stood. They carried heavy loads of dried fish, shells, and occasionally otter skins, in nets slung across their backs, to exchange for deer hides, acorns, medicines, and tobacco.

Cautious and somewhat shy when they approached a village where they were not sure of the reception they would receive, they were accustomed to lay out some merchandise on mats at the outskirts of the village, as a sign that they were ready to trade, and then wait to see what happened. It can only be surmised with what nervous apprehension they embarked on trading expeditions to Catalina Island. They held the Islanders in great awe and were more than a little afraid of them. Also, there was so much at stake, for they were after the highly prized objects of steatite and luxurious otter skins. Of course it was easier, and more fun, on those days when articles were brought in from the Island, or the inland villages, and the trading took place on home ground.

In addition to straight barter of articles, they used a form of money as a medium of exchange. The currency consisted of strings of clam shells, cut one-half inch thick, which were assigned monetary value according to their length. The standard unit was the "ponko" or the measurement of length "from the base to the tip of the middle finger, thence around the outside of the hand past the wrist, back to the point of the middle finger, then once more not quite to the wrist." This complex unit of measurement can be translated roughly as being about thirty inches.

In early Spanish colonial days, an exchange rate existed for "ponkos" and Spanish reales. Four "ponkos" were evaluated as equivalent to one real, or one-eighth of the Spanish dollar. Later the Americans called the real a "bit" and placed its value at about twelve and one-half cents in U.S. currency. So when we say something costs "two bits," we mean eight "ponkos" in Gabrielino money!

After a busy, productive day, when the sun dipped toward the shining, iridescent sea, and the cliffs shaded from tawny gold to vibrant rose, it was time for the men to return from their work. Throughout the villages, the women started preparations for the evening meal. Hundreds of cook fires were kindled, ready to barbecue meat or the shellfish which the women themselves had gathered. The fires would also be needed, of course, to cook the seed-mush, which was always a mainstay of the daily menu. Most of the women of the Peninsula were fortunate in having excellent pots and pans made from the steatite, or soapstone, imported from Catalina Island. These were really superior utensils. It was almost impossible for food to burn in them and, if broken, they could easily be mended with asphaltum.

If, as frequently happened, the men were out on the sea and failed to return before darkness fell, great signal fires were built along the shore to guide them home. And there was undoubtedly much rejoicing when they finally arrived. After the evening meal, the women tidied up, burying the food remains in the communal rubbish heap, cleansing the cooking and eating utensils with brushes made of Yucca fiber, and carefully placing them upside down to protect them until they were used again. Then, if the air was balmy and perchance the moon god, Wiyot, shone down beneficently upon the village, the clan would gather to enjoy the rest of the evening, the women rolling skeins of fiber or stringing beads, the men smoking their steatite pipes and telling wondrous tales about the earth and heavens, and the children, sitting on the outskirts of the circle, listening in rapt attention.

For the men, the main routine of fishing, hunting, boating, and trading was frequently broken by the not unpleasant task of gathering in the temescal, or sweathouse, to help settle affairs of government. The political structure of the Gabrielino community might be described as a limited monarchy. The government of a village, or in rare instances a group of villages, was under the rule of a Chief, who was the acknowledged leader of the dominant clan.

The Chief had heavy responsibilities and commensurate prerogatives. He was a man of wealth, to whom his people were required to give "gifts." But, in turn, he was obligated to dispense large quantities of food and property to visiting officials and guests on public occasions. He was the only man permitted to have more than one wife but his wives had to spend much time gathering property for him to give away. It actually was considered a virtue for him to impoverish himself.

Among the peaceable Gabrielinos warfare was infrequent but deadly. No quarter was given; the wounded were dispatched on the field, usually by decapitation, and the women and children were taken as slaves. Engagements were fought not for conquest, but for affronts believed to have been suffered, sometimes generations earlier. The decision to make war, like all other political decisions, was made in the Council. Then, on the appointed day, the official crier gave the signal for mobilization and onset of action.

Practically the whole village marched out to war, the young men close behind the Chief, followed by the old men, with the women and children bringing up the rear. The women had an important part to play. For days beforehand, they had prepared great quantities of seed-meal mush which they now carried in big bowls to feed the men. Also, during the actual engagements, they and the children had responsibility for gathering the enemy arrows which had missed their targets and delivering them to the fighters on their own side.

Besides "real" warfare, which fortunately was not frequent, the Gabrielinos had the rather amusing custom of verbal wars. For these they composed songs, of the most indecent and obscene language imaginable, against the enemy. Then, once a year, for eight days they would sing and dance against each other, stamping on the ground to express the pleasure they would derive from tramping on the graves of their foes. These "song fights" were relatively harmless and certainly afforded excellent safety valves.

Because Gabrielinos were a people of warm, familial relationships, there was among them a good deal of what today would be called togetherness. Many hours of family endeavor were devoted to production of the carefully wrought articles they made for everyday use, as well as for ceremonial purposes. These arts and crafts are a testimony to their skill and appreciation for aesthetic values, and certainly rank among the finest found in any part of the world.

Out of chert, a stone sometimes referred to as Palos Verdes opal and quite prevalent on the Peninsula, they fashioned ceremonial knives of perfectly symmetrical proportions with an edge as straight and true as a line drawn by a ruler. These knives were often eight to twelve inches in length, an inch in width and not more than an eighth of an inch in thickness. To them wooden handles were affixed with asphaltum.

All of their hunting implements were painstakingly made. Arrowpoints were meticulously carved from chert, then attached to long, graceful cane arrows, which had been made straight and true by carefully running the shaft through the groove of a piece of heated steatite. Fishhooks were exquisitely shaped from the lining of abalone shells, for which the technical name is *Haliotis*. Their implements for making these objects were bits of bone or stone, sharpened into awls, scrapers, and cutting tools.

The Gabrielinos also were excellent basketmakers. These baskets were used for a multitude of purposes: harvesting, seed beating, winnowing, parching, cooking, and even as water bottles. They also made elaborate ceremonial baskets, replete with designs of remarkable beauty, and dyed in patterns of yellow, brown, and black. The dyes, usually obtained in trade, were extracted from plants. A good yellow dye was made from the roots of the Barberry plant. Black was achieved by burying the material to be used for the period of time required for the color change to take place.

A great many of the objects created by the Gabrielinos were made for pure enjoyment, for adornment, or because they had religious significance. Out of steatite, they carved delicate representations of all creatures of the land, sea, and air. Of course, they had every possible variety of beads and their pipes were beautifully turned. It was a custom with them to store their small treasures in abalone shells, cemented together with asphaltum. One of these unique treasure chests may be seen, intact, at the Southwest Museum, in Highland Park, Los Angeles, alongside of an X-ray picture of its contents.

Life for the Gabrielino was not without its measure of fun and excitement. Throughout the year there were numerous social functions and religious celebrations. Weddings were important occasions, and marriages were governed by strict tribal customs. Although usually the alliance began with a spontaneous attraction between the couple, a formal agreement was entered into by the two families and a payment made to the family of the bride, an interesting reversal of the European dowry system.

It was the custom for the prospective bridegroom to spend a period of time, preceding the ceremony, in the parental home of his fiancee, observing her talents as a homemaker. The wedding ceremony itself consisted of a procession leading or carrying the bride to her new home, which had to be in the village of her husband's father, and where her bridegroom sat alone awaiting her. Here the guests who had been officially invited to arrange and carry out the ceremony had the privilege of divesting the bride of her finery as payment for their efforts. The newlyweds were then left alone, while the guests went about the festivities of dancing, singing, and feasting.

Divorce was recognized among the Gabrielinos for two reasons, barrenness and incompatibility; however, instead of the husband having to pay alimony, he was reimbursed his marriage payment. Not a people to be easily discouraged, the woman's family usually began immediately to plan a new marriage. Although, in theory, infidelity was punished by death, in practice, there was simply an exchange of spouses, inasmuch as the wronged husband had the right to take the wife of the other man.

As the Gabrielinos were deeply religious people, many of their social functions took the form of elaborate religious ceremonies. Very complex rituals were held to initiate the boys and girls to mature status in the community. Held separately, of course, these affairs continued for days or even weeks and were extremely expensive. In order to economize on the cost of the fees to officials and of the large amount of food and gifts required, it was customary to wait until a group of candidates were ready for the rite before it was held.

The initiation ceremony for boys started with several days of rigid fasting, followed by their partaking of a highly intoxicating drink, which also had a narcotic effect. It was brewed from the Jimson Weed, a beautiful, poisonous plant that grows in dry waste places over much of Southern California. A large, ceremonial mortar, kept buried at all other times, was used to prepare and serve the beverage.

It did not take long, during the dancing that then ensued, for the potent drink to take effect on the boys. One by one, they fell into a stupor, and having been carefully placed in secluded spots by their adult sponsors, spent the night in dream-filled sleep. For days this ritual was repeated, dancing by day to music made on the deerbone flute, sleeping by night under the influence of the Jimson Weed concoction.

Fantastically cruel methods were used to test the boys' bravery and readiness to enter manhood. At the end of the ordeal, each of them was branded, by setting fire to a patch of dry, combustible leaves, usually on the upper right arm. The resultant scar was an essential symbol of acceptance in the Gabrielino society, and any man who lacked this sign was considered to be a weakling and utterly unfit.

Initiation rites for girls entering womanhood ranked in importance with those held for boys. For them, however, the occasion had much more the flavor of a debut, a joyous presentation to society of a marriageable young woman. Each girl was literally baked for three days in a pit, where she lay on a sort of mattress, constructed from the branches of aromatic plants, over a bed of hot stones. Although she was required to fast during this period, she drank and was bathed with warm water, and was the center of hours of dancing, singing, and distributing of gifts and food.

A sacred ground-painting was made for the girls' ceremony, too, and lectures were given, informing them about how to conduct themselves in order to be popular. They were reminded to bathe daily and were advised to be industrious and hospitable, not become gadabouts, and to maintain a straightforward manner. The celebration was concluded by the girls' having their faces painted by the visiting officials in charge of the ceremony.

Of all the religious ceremonies of the Gabrielinos, those commemorating the dead were considered to be the most important. Great respect was shown to the departed, with specific grounds set aside for burials. Cremation was the general practice, and memorial rites lasting eight days were held once a year, in autumn. These were solemn, but anything but morbid occasions, involving a strict protocol for the treatment of visiting dignitaries, a complex exchange of gifts and fees, and a traditional cycle of singing and dancing.

To a large extent, the open simplicity and tranquility of the Gabrielinos were due to the depth and sincerity of their religious faith. Almost everything they did was governed by the precepts of their religion, which was based on belief in an all-powerful, all-seeing Being, who had created heaven and earth, and who had laid down specific rules regulating the behavior of his creations. Far from feeling restricted by these rules, they enjoyed a deep sense of security and well-being.

Those who lived on what was later to be the Rancho de los Palos Verdes had an especially ideal existence, with a perfect natural setting and much opportunity for indulging their disposition towards sociability. It is believed that there were probably as many as ten villages within this area, which would have provided a fair field for endless visiting back and forth among friendly tribesmen.

It is known that village sites were carefully chosen so as to satisfy two prime requisites: an ample supply of water and safety from winter floods. This meant that they had to be located on high ground and near a lake, a ciénaga, or the mouth of a canyon. These guiding principles have been demonstrated in the location of sites discovered through archeological excavation, as well as in evidence of human habitation uncovered by laymen.

The best known of the sites discovered on the Peninsula is the one at Malaga Cove on a bluff about 223 feet above the ocean. It was partially excavated by the Southwest Museum in 1936, and a report of the findings then made was published. Here were found four well-defined, stratified cultural levels of human habitation. It is believed that the deepest cultural level uncovered was of great antiquity. David Banks Rogers, the well-known archeologist, stated that it was the oldest he had ever observed, and Dr. W. P. Woodring, of the United States Geological Survey, identified the age of the detritus layer in which it was found as late Pleistocene.

The principal artifacts of this ancient people, disclosed through the excavation, were shells and microliths. As the thousands of shells uncovered were not calcined, it was deduced that they must have consumed large quantities of raw shellfish. It was also apparent from the appearance of the shells that they were used as bowls and cutlery as well as for ornamentation. The microliths, averaging five-eights of an inch in length, were made of chert, and were probably used in drilling, cutting, and tattooing.

Apparently a considerable length of time elapsed after the departure of the shellfish people before the next cultural settlement took place, as their village site gave evidence of being greatly weatherbeaten and was deeply scored with cracks. Excavation at this level revealed a markedly different type of culture. The principal artifacts discovered were perfectly made manos and metates (flat grinding stones), indicating that the diet of these people consisted mainly of seed, acorns, and roots. Since no hunting gear and few mammal bones were recovered, evidently hunting was a minor part of their economy.

In sharp contrast, at the next higher level of the excavation there was found an abundance of bones of sea lion, fur seal, sea otter, porpoise, deer, coyote, and rabbit. Also, instead of manos and metates large stone mortars and pestles were found. Among other items uncovered were bone harpoon barbs, exquisitely made fishhooks of abalone shell, and great quantities of fishbones.

At the top layer of the excavation, there was a startling evidence of cultural evolution. Here, for the first time, were found arrowpoints, usually made of chert, but occasionally of chalcedony. Also found were bone flakers, undoubtedly used to make the arrowpoints, and steatite arrowshaft straighteners. Another distinguishing artifact was the highly refined baskethopper mortar. Finally, at the very top, were found some small glass trade beads of the type introduced by the Spaniards at the beginning of the 19th century.

It was apparent to specialists that there was much additional information of great value to be recovered at this remarkable site. Unfortunately, work was postponed, first by World War II and then by lack of funds, and, in 1955, bulldozers moved into the area to make streets and drains for a subdivision, destroying forever any opportunity for further study. Residents of the large condominium, now occupying the site, might like occasionally to think back, over the thousands of years, to the time when long-vanished civilizations lived in the place where they now dwell.

A sense of immediacy could be lent to these reveries by the fact that in 1961, while installing a tennis court, the owner of property adjoining the site found several artifacts on his grounds. These discoveries triggered a three-month study by representatives of the Southwest Museum and two local colleges, resulting in the recovery of over 500 artifacts and three burials. The new site, referred to as Malaga Cove II, was placed as pre-European contact culture and a place of long continuous habitation.

Myriads of additional artifacts and remains have been uncovered over the years, both by trained archeologists and by laymen. From discoveries such as these, and from the intensive work of such well-known experts on Indian culture as Hugo Reid and John Peabody Harrington, the existence of numerous sites and several villages has been established. The precise location of these villages, as well as their Indian names, must remain conjecture based on data gathered through the close, confidential relationships which men like Reid and Harrington had with the last descendents of the Gabrielinos.

Probably the best known of the village sites, after Malaga Cove, is that of Suangna, which meant "Place of the Rushes." This was a large and important rancheria, remnants of which still existed into the 1850s. Tradition places it overlooking old Machado Lake, on the northeast slope of the hills above what is now Anaheim Street, between Gaffey and the Harbor Freeway. Adjacent to Suangna, it is believed, was another village called Masaunga, second "Place of the Rushes." Certainly it is established fact that the area was heavily populated.

Clustered around San Pedro Bay was a group of at least six villages believed to have been ruled by one Chief. It is easy to understand why this area was covered with wickiups and swarming with busy, happy residents. Several deep canyons could have provided an ample water supply, the bay was undoubtedly a center for fishing and boating activities, and the hills offered numerous possible locations for villages on high, protected ground. Although it is impossible to determine even approximate locations for these settlements, bits and pieces of information have been woven into some educated guesses.

It is believed that Tsauvingna was located about where the original town of San Pedro was built, above what Cabrillo called the "Bay of Smokes," and that Xuxungna, the village of the ruling Chief, was on the shore below it. It is surmised that Kingkingna, which might be translated, "Houses by the Sea," must have been on the Bay, and that between this village and the one called Harasngna, was a place which had an "old, old name," Ataviangna. Here a great cemetery once existed.

There is strong archeological evidence to support placement of the village called Munikangna, "The Place of the Small-Large Hill," on the hills above the present intersection of Channel and Gaffey, and a very large kitchen midden, or refuse heap, twelve inches deep, was discovered at Gaffey and 23rd Street. It is also believed that a populous village once existed at Whites Point, but its name is not known.

The presence of ideal living conditions, as well as the discovery of remains, also points to the possibility of village sites at the present location of the Palos Verdes Reservoir and at Portuguese Bend. During construction of a parking lot west of Portuguese Point, a large kitchen midden was found and numerous items uncovered. Among these were shell beads, broken mortars, a pipe, several skulls and a nearly complete skeleton. In the same area, two additional skeletons, one of an adult and the other of a child, were unearthed by gardeners while planting a tree.

Undoubtedly, there still is much valuable information about the culture of early man in California buried beneath the soil of the Rancho de los Palos Verdes. Unfortunately, rapid progress in the development of the Peninsula, with bulldozers moving into new areas on almost a monthly basis, will soon close off this rich fund of potential knowledge. To the layman a collection of mortars and pestles or other relics doesn't appear to be too important, a temporary conversation piece perhaps, but not a possible key to the way of life of a long-vanished people.

Generations of collectors, some genuinely scientific in spirit, others merely "pot-hunters," have already denuded vast areas of quantities of valuable material. Since only the specialist can evaluate the importance of a discovery, the greatest contribution the amateur collector can make is to handle all materials found with consummate care and turn them over as soon as possible, to the staff of a college or university with a program in archeology, or to the Southwest Museum. In this way the long search into the past can be continued, and who can predict what startling finds are yet to be made.

So the memory of the quiet people of the chaparral, the first inhabitants of the Rancho de los Palos Verdes, may be preserved. And out of the mists of time, the spirit of their serenity and gentle mysticism may influence the lives of those who now dwell on the terraced hills and among the sheltering coves.

2

From Distant Shores

JUST WHEN THE FIRST emissaries of a foreign civilization sighted the land of California may never be a certainty. There are tales still told of Buddhist monks who in their voyaging came upon "an island 4000 miles in circumference on which grows a tree 20,000 feet high whose fruit makes men immortal." Allowing for some exaggeration, the island might have been California, and the tree could have been the magnificent redwood. Certainly the great Chinese ships of the 12th century were capable of sailing across the Pacific, as were the giant outriggers of the Polynesians. It also has been suggested that Indian legends about blond sea gods had their origin in visitations from the fleet of Alexander the Great during the third century B.C.

Intriguing as surmises may be, it is established fact that the eyes of the first European to behold the beauty of the California coastline were those of Juan Rodríguez Cabrillo. It is also known that on this historic voyage he sailed into San Pedro Bay and skirted the hills of the Palos Verdes Peninsula.

To appreciate how he came to be within a stone's throw of the sand dunes of what is now Cabrillo Beach on that Sunday morning of October 8, 1542, it is necessary to back up about twenty years to the time when

Cabrillo arrived in Veracruz, Mexico, as a soldier sent in an expedition to castigate the overly ambitious and proud conquistador, Hernań Cortés.

Cabrillo was then probably in his late twenties, already cast in the mold of his era—courageous, capable, even ruthless. Born in Spain, he had come to the New World as a youth and experienced military service in the conquest of Cuba. By the time he landed on the humid, tropical shore of Veracruz, he was well versed in the skills of mariner and merchant-adventurer. Soon he would find himself in the service of the man he had come to humiliate.

Cortés had arrived in Mexico in 1519, commander of the armada deployed by Diego Velázquez, then Governor of Cuba, to exploit the potential riches of the mainland. From the beginning of their association there had been friction between the two men, as Cortés repeatedly flaunted his insubordination. Now, after waging a bloody campaign through the Mexican provinces, Cortés marched on Tenochtitlán, capital of the great Aztec empire, and captured the fabled golden city. Meanwhile, Velázquez seethed with outrage over reports that Cortés had found immense treasure and was petitioning the King of Spain to give him independent domain in the conquered territory. Finally, he decided to deal with him, dispatching an army, led by Pánfilo de Narváez, to punish the recalcitrant commander.

To meet the threat from Narváez, Cortés left his newly made conquest in the charge of a trusted lieutenant and marched forth with a portion of his own army. Though vastly outnumbered, he encountered little difficulty in defeating the invaders, who were ill trained and overconfident. Most of them were only too willing to join forces with him, lured by glittering promises of riches and prestige. Cabrillo was among those who came into his camp.

Triumphantly, Cortés returned to Tenochtitlán to find that serious conflict had been precipitated with the once seemingly docile Aztecs, now determined to oust the hated Spaniards. Forced to make a hasty evacuation, Cortés tried to take as much treasure as possible. This proved disastrous. Overburdened with heavy loads of silver and gold, the Spanish soldiers were easy targets for the infuriated Indians, who cut them to pieces. During one desperate night, Cortés lost sixty-five per cent of his men. Cabrillo was one of the survivors.

He was destined to play a key role in the reconquest and final subjugation of the Aztec nation, which was accomplished through a unique amphibious operation carried out on the great lake that surrounded

Tenochtitlán. It was a type of warfare similar to that used by the United States Marines in the Pacific theater more than 400 years later. Cabrillo had prime responsibility for building the thirteen brigantines, the principal strategic means for destruction of the Aztecs' fabulous city of temples and palaces. Several years later, this experience was to stand him in good stead, when he embarked on his own shipbuilding career in Guatemala.

Meanwhile he spent two to three years as a member of expeditions which conquered the rest of Mexico and most of Central America. Culminating his conquistadorial career, in 1524 under the command of Pedro de Alvarado, he was one of the founders of the capital of Guatemala. He was about to reap the rewards of the arduous effort and dangerous activity to which he had devoted himself in the service of Spain.

High honors were bestowed upon him and he was given several huge grants of land. He married the sister of a fellow conquistador, established a beautiful home, and started a family. As the right-hand man of Alvarado, now Governor of Spain's new empire in Central America, he had boundless opportunities for acquiring a great personal fortune. He engaged in both shipbuilding and mining operations, achieving a position of impressive wealth and prestige.

Then, in 1536, Alvarado decided that he wanted to build a large fleet of ships that could be sent out to explore the still unknown vast reaches of the Pacific. Cabrillo joined him in the venture, investing a sizable share of his fortune and much of his time. The construction of the fleet was a long, hard, complicated task, and the work proceeded intermittently over a number of years.

Finally the fleet stood ready, three galleons of 200 tons each, seven ships of 100 tons, and three smaller vessels. On Christmas Day, 1540, they were a beautiful sight, sailing into the harbor at Navidad, Mexico.

But complications and red tape impeded the start of an expedition. Don Antonio Mendoza, the Viceroy of Mexico, who wanted to be cut in on the enterprise, withheld his approval. He and Alvarado were unable to come to an agreement; the months dragged on. Then tragedy struck. Alvarado, called to assist in suppressing an Indian insurrection, was killed by a falling horse.

Cabrillo faced Mendoza alone, with a substantial investment at stake. At last, after much hedging and many more delays, Mendoza took full possession of the fleet, but permitted Cabrillo to remain in command and consented to let him sail with two of the ships, the *Victoria* and the *San Salvador*. So it was that on June 27, 1542, Cabrillo, then in his early forties, sailed north from Navidad on the expedition that was to bring him to the shores of the Palos Verdes Peninsula. He was never to return from his voyage.

The main purpose of the expedition was to find the mythical Straits of Anián, or Northwest Passage between the Pacific and the Atlantic, in which the Spaniards so stubbornly and so long believed. The ships were sturdy and sound, of the caravel, or round ship type, similar to those of Columbus.

They sailed up the coast of Mexico, across the Gulf of California, then north along the shores of Baja California. The weather was good, but inasmuch as they progressed only about 15 to 20 miles a day, anchoring during the night, it took them better than two and a half months to reach Ensenada, where they stayed for five days.

On Friday, September 22, the expedition pushed on to explore the unknown coast to the north. Six days later, the *San Salvador* and *Victoria* became the first vessels other than Indian craft to enter the waters of what is now San Diego harbor. Cabrillo was well pleased with the port, describing it as "closed and very good," and naming it San Miguel, in honor of Saint Michael the Archangel.

Taking a party ashore, he encountered the Diegueño Indians, who were "comely and large," but "gave no signs of great fear." A kind of communication was carried on by sign language, and the Indians "told" Cabrillo that inland there were men like those in his party, bearded, clothed, armed, and on horseback, and that they were killing the Indians. Obviously all the Indians in the Southwest had an excellent grapevine, because the white men to which these people referred were undoubtedly those in the Coronado land expedition, which had explored Arizona and New Mexico during the years 1539 to 1541. Cabrillo managed to pacify the natives, giving them presents, and avoided any incidents other than one in which arrows did wound three members of his party.

While the ships were in port, a violent storm came up, but the harbor provided completely adequate protection and no damage was suffered. On Tuesday, October 3, the expedition proceeded up the coast. In the wonderfully clear atmosphere that customarily follows a storm in Southern California, the men were able to observe every detail of the land along which they sailed, noting the "many valleys and plains" as well as "the mountains in the interior."

As dusk began to fall on October 6, they sighted the islands which are now called San Clemente and Santa Catalina, and which they named

Victoria and San Salvador. Because the wind died down, they were unable to reach them that night, but at daybreak on Saturday, the 7th, they anchored off San Salvador, or Catalina Island, and a party started for the shore.

As their boat drew near, a large number of Indians emerged from the bushes "shouting, dancing, and making signs that they should land." These, of course, were the Island Gabrielinos. They showed no signs of being afraid, some of them even putting out in one of their own craft to meet the Spaniards. Cabrillo gave them beads and other gifts, and they remained relaxed and at ease when the Spanish party came ashore for a brief visit. They too "had the word" that there were white men roaming about on the mainland, and they conveyed this information to Cabrillo by signs.

Early Sunday morning, the ships moved into San Pedro Bay. On the Palos Verdes Hills, Cabrillo saw the smoke of many fires and so named the harbor, *Bahía de los Humos,* or Bay of Smokes. What he saw, undoubtedly, were the signal fires of one or more of the Gabrielino villages, perhaps Tsauvigna and Xuxungna, or Harasgna, left burning all night to guide the men of the villages safely home from a fishing foray. Actually, he did encounter a group of Gabrielinos in a canoe and "talked" with them, again learning of other white men in the interior.

So far as is known, Cabrillo made no landing at San Pedro, but, on Monday, resumed his voyage north, circling the shape of the Peninsula. As he spent the day sailing past the mauve and umber tinted hills, with Catalina Island sprawled, pink and purple, across a gleaming channel, and rounded the sheer, towering cliffs above Bluff Cove, he must have been impressed with the beauty he saw. Towards dusk, he came into what he called a large ensenada and anchored in Santa Monica Bay for the night.

From this point on, Cabrillo was dogged by disaster. Proceeding up the coast, he reached the Channel Islands on October 18. He was now surrounded by some of the roughest currents of the California coastline, and the weather had turned ugly. Anchoring at what is now Cuyler Bay on San Miguel Island, the ships were forced to remain for a week. Then, battered by angry seas, they drifted along the coast between Point Conception and Point Reyes, reaching as far north as the Russian River. Here they turned back, and on November 16 they came to the large ensenada which later would be called Monterey Bay, but dared not land because of the high sea and adverse wind. Fighting fresh storms, they proceeded southward along the frighteningly jagged shoreline of the

the Santa Lucia Mountains. It seemed to the terrified sailors that the cliffs "were about to fall on the ships."

Finally, on November 23, the tattered armada reached the Channel Islands, where they chose to wait out the worst of the winter anchored at Santa Catalina Island. Unfortunately, the once friendly Indians became restive at the long visitation and began a series of running skirmishes against the intruders. Then, on Christmas Eve, they attacked a party of soldiers sent ashore for water. Sorely pressed, the men called out to the flagship for help. Cabrillo took it upon himself to lead a landing party to their rescue. Perhaps tired or momentarily careless, he stumbled on a rocky ledge and fell, breaking his leg. Stubbornly he dragged himself ashore and refused to leave the island until all his men were rescued.

Cabrillo was finally taken back aboard ship, but the surgeon was unable to treat the wound satisfactorily. Gangrene soon developed. In agony and aware that death was near, Cabrillo turned his command over to Bartolomé Ferrelo, charging him with responsibility for pushing the expedition on to the north. On January 3, the iron-willed commander died.

Ferrelo did his best to carry out Cabrillo's orders, sailing to the vicinity of the Oregon border before turning back. It was a horrendous voyage. At last, on April 14, 1543, the battered and leaking fleet returned to Navidad, nearly nine months after embarking.

Spain had little use for the accomplishments of the expedition. No Northwest Passage had been found. No treasure had been discovered. At this time, information about an apparently endless coastline appeared to be of slight importance.

No great honors were bestowed upon Cabrillo for discovering California. The seizure of his property and revenues, which had begun almost as soon as he had left Guatemala, was immediately accelerated. Soon his family was reduced to poverty. Years of litigation ensued, carried on by his widow, his sons, and grandsons, before some measure of justice was rendered.

More years went by before Cabrillo received the recognition he deserved. Even the names he gave his discoveries were erased from the maps. But today the memory of his courage and accomplishment is kept alive in the many landmarks which bear his name. It is appropriate that some of these are on the Palos Verdes Peninsula, where his brief encounter was a pleasant one.

Not long after Cabrillo's death, an event occurred which was soon to change Spain's indifferent attitude toward California. In 1559, the first successful trading expedition between Acapulco and Manila was accomplished, and the renowned tradition of the Manila Galleon, which was to persist for 250 years, came into being.

The great sailing vessels made annual voyages across the Pacific, laden with gold and silver which they exchanged for the fabulous treasures of the Far East. The outward-bound trip from Acapulco presented few problems. With favorable winds, the voyage could be accomplished in about three months. Coming back was an entirely different matter.

The galleons were loaded with riches from Indonesia, China, Japan, and India; tons of ivory, jade and jewels, china and porcelain, spices and exotic foods, silks and rugs, camphor and sandalwood. Creaking under these tremendous loads, the ships were not easy to maneuver, and it was a tricky job just to get through the archipelago and out into the open sea. Then there was the problem of catching the right currents to make the long run across the ocean. When land was sighted in the vicinity of Cape Mendocino, there was still the hard pull down to Acapulco.

With luck, the trip averaged about seven months. During this time, there was a constant threat of vicious storms or typhoons, radical changes in temperature, and no fresh water or food. As a rule, by the time the galleons reached the California coast, most of the crews were ill from scurvy and other diseases. There was a desperate need for a port of call, where supplies could be picked up.

There was a second reason why such a haven was needed. As the years went by, and the news of the treasure-laden galleons got around the world, they became fair game for freebooters. English pirates, like Sir John Hawkins and Sir Francis Drake, made tremendous hauls hijacking the huge ships, and this with the tacit approval of the brilliantly quixotic and aggressive first Elizabeth of England.

In 1579, El Dragón, as the Spanish described Drake, not only lifted millions of dollars worth of goods from the galleons in the Pacific, but also went up the west coast at least as far as Cabrillo's expedition had, searching for the short-cut passage between the Pacific and the Atlantic in which everyone still firmly believed. Landing at what is today called Drake's Bay, he took possession of all of California in the name of Queen Elizabeth. This proved too much for Spain to swallow.

Suddenly Spain's interest in California revived. It was determined that if anyone was to discover a Northwest Passage or establish settlements along the route of the galleons, it should be Spain. The galleon commanders were instructed to search the coast on their return voyages, both for the mythical strait and for a port. Records exist to substantiate brief visitations to California by a number of captains toward the end of the sixteenth century. Finally an expedition embarked specifically for the purpose of surveying the California coast and locating good harbors. The commander was Sebastián Vizcaíno.

Vizcaíno was a robust, energetic man of about fifty, who had been reared to the sea in the tradition of a soldier from the Basque provinces. After coming to Mexico, he had invested heavily in the galleon trade and was a logical choice for his assignment, as he had lost a fortune when the vessel, the *Santa Ana* was hijacked off Baja California by the English pirate, Cavendish. On the other hand, there were misgivings about his capabilities to carry out the venture.

Condé de Monterey, the Viceroy of New Spain, expressed his doubts in a letter to the king in which he wrote that it "seemed to me, with regard to the person, his quality and capital are not sufficient in connection with an enterprise of such vast importance." In the end, he *was* given command of the expedition, but under strict controls and detailed instruction, most of which he disregarded.

He sailed from Acapulco, in May, 1602, with about 200 men, on two fairly well-equipped ships, the *San Diego* and the *Santo Tomás,* and a small frigate, the *Tres Reyes.* He was instructed to explore carefully from the tip of Baja California to Cape Mendocino for possible shelters from storms, but to establish no settlements, and under no circumstances to change the names of landmarks already on the maps. By the time the expedition reached Cabrillo's port of San Miguel on November 12, many of the men were already ill, due to a serious shortage of water. Possibly it was an indication of Vizcaíno's incompetence that the ships' water barrels had been made of worn-out wood. There can be no question that he was delinquent in following specific orders when he took it upon himself to rename San Miguel as San Diego.

The fleet stayed in this port long enough for the crews to recover and then sailed north, skirting the coast. On the 24th of November, three islands were sighted. As it was the eve of the feast of Santa Catalina, Vizcaíno named the largest one after the saint. Later he gave the name San Clemente to the one farther to the southwest. These, of course, were the San Salvador and Victoria of Cabrillo, and so showed on Vizcaíno's map. It seems strange that he failed to assign a name to the one unnamed island, the one later to be called San Nicolas.

Experiencing some difficulty reaching the islands because of an adverse headwind, the ships headed first towards the mainland. The smoke from many fires and green vegetation on the hills of the Palos Verdes Peninsula attracted them, but as they approached the bay to its southeast end, Vizcaíno evaluated the harbor as having insufficient protection from the wind. He renamed the bay, which Cabrillo had called *Bahía de los Humos,* San Pedro, as it was the 26th of November, the feast day of Saint Peter. Once again he had disobeyed orders.

On the morning of the 27th, the expedition entered what is now Avalon Bay. A large number of Indians came out in canoes to greet them, boarding the foreign ships quite fearlessly, and giving signs of great welcome. Once again, as they had with Cabrillo, the hospitable Gabrielinos of the Islands guided the ships into the harbor and urged the men to come ashore. Vizcaíno and a small party went on the beach and were immediately treated to delicacies such as roasted sardines and small fruits that tasted like sweet potatoes. In return they gave their hosts pieces of clothing and beads.

The next day, the Spaniards built a small hut on the beach and said Mass. More than 150 Indians came to see the wondrous spectacle, marveling at the altar and the image of the crucified Christ. With signs, they asked what it was all about. When told it was about Heaven, they marveled even more. Deeply religious, the Gabrielinos were intensely interested. After the service, the Indian women invited Vizcaíno into their houses, leading him by the hand and giving him food. They were treating him, according to their tradition, as they would any guest.

There was no protest when he took several of the young girls, ranging in age from eight to ten years, on board his ship. Most of the women followed in canoes, and everyone was very happy with the gifts they received from the Spanish: chemises, petticoats, and necklaces. In return the Indians gave generously of otter skins, shells, nets, thread, and rope. But unfortunately they created the impression of being thieves, as they helped themselves to goods which they saw lying around. It is remarkable that this appears to have been the only point of misunderstanding between two such completely different cultures.

While part of the fleet was anchored at the Isthmus, a small boat was put to sea to reconnoitre. It came upon another island, the one later to be called Dead Man's Island, in San Pedro Bay. There eight Indians came out in a canoe and indicated by signs that there were men inland, bearded and clothed like the Spaniards. By the time the launch returned with this information, a dense fog had set in and the weather had turned very cold. Worried about the illness among his crews and the almost certain advent of winter storms, Vizcaíno decided to waste no more time exploring, but to sail on at once in order to insure completion of the voyage.

On Sunday, December 1, with thick fog obscuring any view of the Palos Verdes Peninsula, the ships moved northward. This was the last time for well over 150 years that a European ship was to come close enough to enter the waters of San Pedro Bay. Once more the "huge houses on the sea" with their great white sails were to become a legend with the Gabrielinos, possibly reinforced each year by the glimpse of a galleon sailing past.

Vizcaíno proceeded past Point Conception and the Santa Lucia Mountains and anchored at Cabrillo's Bay of Pines, which he named Monterey, in honor of the Viceroy of New Spain, a shrewd political move. From there, in order to reduce demands on his dwindling supplies, he sent the sick back to Acapulco on the *Santo Tomás*. By the time that ship reached Mexico, twenty-five men had died. Meanwhile the *San Diego* and the *Tres Reyes* pushed on through a furious south wind, accompanied by blinding fog and rain.

The voyage was fraught with immense hardships. Suffering and loss of life were horrible. Only six crewmen were alive when the *Tres Reyes* arrived in Navidad. The *San Diego* fared little better.

With an enormous cost in human lives, Vizcaíno had accomplished no more than Cabrillo had, sixty years before, except that he carefully recorded the results of his expedition. Ironically, Spain once again did nothing to follow up on what had been discovered.

3

Explorers Become Settlers

AN INTERVAL OF A CENTURY AND A HALF elapsed before steps were taken to utilize the ports of Alta California. As so frequently happens in the affairs of men, the Manila Galleons, for whose safety the explorations had originally been undertaken, chose to head directly for Acapulco once they reached the California coast. Apparently, it was of little value to them to have a port of call unless the sanctuary of a colony also existed, and the establishment of permanent settlements appeared to be impractical so long as the only way to bring supplies for their support was by a long and hazardous sea voyage. When the momentous decision to found a colony was finally made, late in 1768, it was the result of the converging of three distinct forces.

One of the most powerful influences in the affairs of New Spain was the Catholic Church. Due to the zeal of tireless and courageous men like the Friars Eusebio Francisco Kino and Juan María Salvatierra, the frontiers of the Spanish empire were gradually pushed northwestward until, by the middle of the eighteenth century, they extended in a great arc from Louisiana to Baja California, where thirteen missions had been established. The good fathers could hardly wait to extend their activities to the heathen in Alta California. When control of the missions passed into the hands of the fervent Father Junípero Serra, with the expulsion

36

of the Jesuits in 1767, the intensity of the campaign for converting the Indians was, if anything, augmented.

At the same time, the threat of foreign encroachment rose again to trouble the Spanish government. Discovery of the valuable sea otter brought both the Russians and the English into Pacific waters. In the early 1700s, representatives of the Russian Czar laid claim to the Aleutian Islands and soon developed an extremely profitable trade in otter skins with China. This eventually resulted in establishment of the Russian American Fur Company and the founding of Fort Ross in Northern California. Meanwhile, the English, who were causing Spain considerable concern with their colonization of the Atlantic seaboard, got wind of the otter trade and were poaching along the Pacific coast. It was time to act.

At this moment, the third force converged. In 1765, Charles III of Spain appointed as ruler of the Kingdom of New Spain, José de Gálvez. Gálvez was a man of iron will, a skilled statesman, energetic and imaginative, and ambitious almost to the point of megalomania. Among the many enterprises which engaged his attention when he took office, nothing interested him as much as developing the resources of Alta California. Three years after his appointment, he had completed arrangements for establishing a colony at San Diego.

In the expedition organized to accomplish this feat were two soldiers destined to play a very important role in the history of the Rancho de los Palos Verdes. One was Lieutenant Pedro Fages, who was to become the fourth governor of California; the other was Juan José Domínguez, who was to receive the first land grant in Alta California from Fages. The grant was Rancho San Pedro, almost half of which was to become the Rancho de los Palos Verdes. It is quite likely that the two men met for the first time in San Diego, when the sea and land divisions of the expedition came together there.

Three vessels were outfitted for the sea part of the expedition: the *San Carlos,* the *San Antonio,* and the *San José.* Under the command of Vicente Vila, the *San Carlos* sailed first, leaving La Paz on January 9, 1769. On board were sixty-two persons, including Lieutenant Pedro Fages and his company of twenty-five Catalonian volunteers. From the start, the ship met only misfortune.

The haul up the coast was difficult at best because of adverse winds. To further complicate the situation, the expedition encountered winter storms and fog. But the worst thing that happened was the outbreak of an epidemic. Early in the voyage, due to leaking water casks, the water supply ran out. A stop was made at Cedros Island where unfortunately the water taken was from a brackish stream and polluted. The resultant illness added to the ravages already being made among the men by scurvy. Soon there were no sailors left with sufficient strength to work the vessel. Then, to cap the series of misadventures, the ship got lost.

Guided by latitudes given by the early explorers, which were far from exact, and blinded by fog, the *San Carlos* passed by the harbor at San Diego and entered San Pedro Bay. Unfortunately, Vila made no attempt to land, as undoubtedly the friendly Gabrielinos would have provided him with fresh supplies. Pushing on as far as the Channel Islands, he finally turned back and came into San Diego, with all hands desperately ill, almost four months after leaving La Paz.

He found the *San Antonio* already safely at anchor, although it had not started its voyage until February 15. Rude tents were made of sail to shelter the sick. The weather was raw and windy, and there was no adequate food or medication. Soon the men from the *San Antonio* were also infected.

For two weeks, every day two or three men died in the canvas pesthouses, and the few who managed to stay well had their hands full caring for the sick and burying the dead. The eagerly awaited third vessel, the *San José,* never appeared. At last, on May 14, when only about sixteen soldiers and sailors of the original ninety members of the expedition were still alive, the first division of the land contingent arrived. It can easily be imagined with what joy they were received.

This division, under the command of Rivera y Moncada, had been en route for fifty-one days. In the party was the well-known Fray Juan Crespi, former student and long-time friend of Father Junípero Serra, forty-two Christian Indians, several muleteers, and twenty-five *soldados de cuero,* or leather-jacket troops, from the royal Presidio of Loreto. The leather-jackets derived their name from the sleeveless leather coat made of white deerskin which they wore as protection against the Indian arrows. They were tough, hard-bitten veterans of the frontier, resolute and fearless, and the best horsemen in the world. One of these *soldados de cuero* was Juan José Domínguez.

Domínguez was then about thirty-three years old. He had already had thirteen years of hard military service in the desolate northern province of Mexico and Baja California. Arriving in San Diego, after weeks of arduous travel on scant rations, he shared in the bitter disappointment of his fellow soldiers at not finding the provisions to which they had looked forward. But he, along with everyone else, devoted complete attention to caring for the sick and trying to build the rudiments of a settlement. In the ensuing six weeks of grim hardship, before the second division of the land expedition arrived, it is quite possible that Fages, the young cavalry officer, and Domínguez, the experienced and reliable soldier, struck up a fast friendship.

On June 29, the remainder of the overland expedition came into the destitute camp, bringing with them several hundred head of cattle and a pack train. Leading this contingent were Don Gaspar De Portolá, overall commander of the project, and the renowned Father Serra. A royal presidio was established and, within two weeks, on the eve of the founding of the Mission San Diego, Portolá took off for Monterey with a major portion of the able-bodied men. He was determined to carry out the rest of Visitador-General Gálvez's instructions and locate the port so highly praised by Vizcaíno. In the party that headed north were Lieutenant Pedro Fages and Juan José Domínguez.

Their route was roughly along the coast and then inland through La Brea Canyon and across the San Gabriel Valley to a site on the Los Angeles River, which Portolá named *Nuestra Señora la Reina de Los Angeles de Porciúncula*. Here the party camped overnight on the place, where twelve years later, the Pueblo of Los Angeles was to be founded. They then proceeded across what is now known as Hancock Park, through the Santa Monica Mountains and San Fernando Valley, and into the rugged Santa Susana Range, emerging on the coast near present day Ventura. Once again they hugged the shoreline, until the formidable barrier of the Santa Lucia Mountains forced them inland to where they found and followed the Salinas River to the sands of Monterey.

Now the tragicomedy of the expedition occurred. They failed to recognize Monterey Bay as the place which Vizcaíno had so glowingly described!

After wandering so far north as to sight the Point Reyes Peninsula, and accidentally discovering the Golden Gate on their return, they finally gave up in despair and retraced their weary steps back to San Diego. There, Serra rebuked Portolá for his statement that he couldn't find Monterey, with the cryptic remark, "You come from Rome without having seen the Pope."

Gálvez was no more sympathetic. He ordered Portolá to set off immediately with another expedition. This time a ship was also dispatched bringing Father Serra, and on the afternoon of May 24, 1770, the priest and the soldier met at Monterey. A Presidio was established, and a few days later the Mission of San Cárlos de Borromeo de Monterey was dedicated.

Lieutenant Pedro Fages was privileged to be present at these historic events, but Juan Domínguez had been sent back to Loreto. It is probable that the two men did not meet again for twelve to fourteen years, as by the time Domínguez returned from Mexico, late in 1773, Fages had been removed from his post as Military Commander of Alta California.

During these years, Spanish control of California was expanded principally through the founding of additional missions. The second in Southern California was the Mission San Gabriel Arcángel, from which the Gabrielino Indians derived their name. In September of 1771, a delegation of these Indians from the village of Sibangna came to meet the priests and soldiers, as they arrived to erect the mission, on a lovely wooded spot on the River San Gabriel. Although at first hostile, when one of the priests held up a painting of the Virgin, the Indians threw down their arms and laid their strings of beads at the feet of the image. Then, in their usual friendly fashion, they helped to construct the stockade and buildings and brought offerings of pine nuts and acorns to the altar at which the strangers worshipped.

Within a few years, the Mission San Gabriel was self-sustaining, ranking ahead of all the other missions in stock raising and agricultural production. This was essentially what made it possible to found the Pueblo of Los Angeles, and, a little later, to support several large, private ranchos in what is now the County of Los Angeles.

At the outset of the year 1781, Governor Felipe de Neve ordered the recruitment of prospective settlers for the farming community he wanted to establish on the Los Angeles River. By February 2, a dozen eager recruits were assembled, with their families, in the little mining town of Los Alamos in Sonora. These were courageous paisanos, willing to leave their homes in Mexico and brave the hardships of an unknown country.

Designated to accompany them was a military escort of twelve volunteers, with their wives and children. One of these soldiers was a thirty-nine-year-old man named Francisco Xavier Sepúlveda, and with him was his wife, María Candelaría de Redondo, and six children. The eldest of these was a boy of seventeen, Juan José. He was destined to be the father of the founder of the Rancho de los Palos Verdes.

A thousand-mile journey lay ahead of the brave little company of men, women, and children. After seven long, weary months of travel, across deserts and mountains, they arrived at the San Gabriel Mission on

August 18. There, only twenty miles from their destination, they were quarantined for seventeen days because they had been exposed to smallpox en route. Released on the morning of September 4, they got off to an early start, eager to be on their way.

Trudging along the hot, dusty trail that is now Mission Road, they came to the east bank of the Los Angeles River, which at that time of the year must have been just a rippling stream. Nevertheless, young Juan José eyed it longingly, wishing he could get down into the cool water. But he had to keep up with the party that plodded doggedly beside the river bank, where occasional shade from sycamores and willows relieved the heat from the blazing sun.

The route which they followed is now called Aliso Street. Finally, as the long shadows of late afternoon made patterns of the cottonwood branches on the high ground across the river, they forded the stream and mounted the site where Fages and Domínguez had camped twelve years earlier.

Here a number of friendly but curious Gabrielino Indians, from the village of Yangna, located nearby in the vicinity of the present City Hall, stole forward to watch the strangers. As dusk began to fall, they saw the tired, dusty travelers unpack their mules and start to get settled.

Francisco Xavier Sepúlveda was one of the men who erected a rude temporary shelter of branches and tules on that warm September evening, while María brought water up from the river to cook the evening meal and Juan José gathered wood for the campfire. After a supper of beans and tortillas, the Sepúlveda family, consisting of five boys and one girl sat around the fire and dreamed of a bright future in the new Pueblo de Los Angeles.

It was not long before the drama of events which was to make those dreams a reality began to unfold. The very next year, Juan José Domínguez, who had spent the thirteen years since his adventures with Fages at the Presidios of Loreto, Monterey and in San Diego, decided it was time to retire from military service. After more than a quarter of a century of arduous effort, the forty-six-year-old soldier was ready for a little peace and quiet.

Having been fortunate in acquiring a substantial herd of cattle, he began to look around for a location which would provide good grazing land for his stock. He investigated several possible sites, and became interested in a vast expanse of coastal plain stretching from the Pueblo de Los Angeles to the Pacific Ocean.

On this land, partly covered with a thick tangle of trees and bramble bushes, was adequate water for his herds, and the wide open spaces and terraced hills of the Peninsula provided a huge acreage on which his cattle could feed. He determined to obtain permission to occupy it.

Coincidentally, in September of 1782, Domínguez's old commander and friend, Pedro Fages, returned to San Diego from Mexico as the newly appointed Governor of Alta California. He saw fit to recognize the petition which Domínguez made, and, in 1784, he bestowed upon him the first private land concession in Southern California, the Rancho San Pedro.

Out of this Rancho, a number of years later, was to be carved a huge tract of land, known as the Rancho de los Palos Verdes and given to the son of Juan José Sepúlveda.

Juan José Domínguez was very proud of the princely domain which he had acquired. Covering well over 75,000 acres, it included the present cities of Redondo, Torrance, Compton, Gardena, Lomita, San Pedro, Wilmington, the western side of Long Beach, and, of course, all of the Palos Verdes Peninsula.

Quite possibly, as he rode over the brow of the Palos Verdes Hills, Domínguez was the first European to see from the land side the Peninsula's lovely coves and scalloped shoreline. Undoubtedly he came upon several of the Indian villages in which the Gabrielinos still lived their happy, carefree lives. A new era was about to dawn and a century was drawing to a close.

But before it ended, one last representative of a foreign government was to leave his impress upon the land that now belonged to Domínguez. In November of 1793, a ninety-foot British sloop, the *Discovery,* under the command of George Vancouver, skirted the Peninsula. Vancouver had been sent by King George III, to look after England's interests in Pacific waters and to survey the northwest coast of America.

En route he made two stops along the shores of California. At each place he met a mission father with whom he was deeply impressed. Today the two rugged promontories which bear the names of these two priests are Point Fermin and Point Vicente.

When Vancouver anchored in Monterey Bay, in 1792, he received an exceedingly warm welcome. He was royally entertained at the Presidio, offered every convenience for the repair of his vessels, and generously provided with supplies. On Sunday, December 2, he was invited to visit the Mission of San Cárlos de Borromeo at Carmel. There he met Father Fermín Francisco de Lasuén, the man who had succeeded to the office of President of the Missions shortly after the death of Father Serra.

Vancouver describes the priest, then in his seventies, as one ''whose gentle manners, united to a most venerable and placid countenance, indicated that tranquilized state of mind, that fitted him to an eminent degree for presiding over so benevolent an institution.'' A most pleasant afternoon was spent with the good Father, and Vancouver was never to forget him.

Later, in Santa Barbara, he met Friar Vicente Santa María of the Mission of San Buenaventura. The two men related immediately. Vancouver invited Vicente to accompany him to Buenaventura on his vessel. Of the trip he wrote, ''I had only reason to regret the short time I was to be indulged with the society of a gentleman, whose observations through life, and general knowledge of mankind, rendered him a most pleasing and instructive companion.''

At Ventura Father Vicente, sympathetic to the needs imposed by a long sea voyage, gave generously of supplies from the mission. Four canoes were required to bring on board the sheep, fowl, and vegetables provided. Small wonder that Vancouver was impressed with his friend.

Sailing south, on Sunday, November 24, 1793, Vancouver rounded Point Dume and across Santa Monica Bay sighted ''mountainous country, which had the appearance of being rugged and barren . . . extending towards the sea coast and forming at its extreme point a conspicuous promontory.'' This he named Point Vicente.

Towards evening he came around the southeast side of the Palos Verdes Peninsula to that ''projecting promontory between two bays, the shores of which terminate on all sides in steep cliffs of a light yellowing colour,'' and reached San Pedro Bay. On the headland which guards the west entrance to the bay, he bestowed the name Point Fermín.

As Vancouver sailed past San Pedro Bay, he looked in vain for a place of which he had heard: ''a very advantageous settlement established on a fertile spot somewhere in this neighborhood within sight of the ocean, though at a distance of some miles from the coast, called Pueblo de los Angeles.''

So the last of the emissaries from distant shores came and went from the Palos Verdes Peninsula. The era of the discoverers was ended. The time of the rancheros was about to begin.

4

Two Illustrious Families

THE EARLY HISTORY of the Rancho de los Palos Verdes is the story of a bitter struggle for the land. It is also the story of two of California's most prominent families. Across its pages are indelibly impressed the names—Domínguez and Sepúlveda.

Shortly after receiving his grant to the Rancho San Pedro, Juan José Domínguez moved his cattle north from San Diego and took possession. Camp was made near the river, just east of what is still Domínguez Hill. Indians from the village of Suangna were pressed into service as vaqueros and to help with construction work. For the first time, horses and cattle roamed the Palos Verdes Hills and the rolling land that stretched to the mudflats that were to become Wilmington. Soon huts and stock corrals were silhouetted against the sky.

The first Domínguez ranch house was a crude structure. It consisted of two rooms, with adobe walls and an earthen floor, and measured about thirty-three feet square. Pitch covered the rough roof made of willow branches. It mattered little to Domínguez that his house had few comforts as he had no family and lived there himself only at intervals, spending a good deal of his time at the Pueblo of Los Angeles and on trips to San Diego.

The informal nature of his land concession did not disturb him either, although it was little more than a cattle-grazing permit. This was the way permissions to occupy land were given under the Laws of the Indies. At the same time, in the same way, two of his compadres also received permissions for huge tracts of land: the Rancho Los Nietos given to Manuel Nieto, and the Rancho San Rafael granted to José María Verdugo. Altogether, the three tracts comprised over four thousand square miles and covered almost one-third of the coastal plain now included in Los Angeles County. Yet there were no maps drawn and no actual measurement of the land.

The casualness with which the land transaction was handled resulted in years of litigation and alienation between the Domínguez heirs and the Sepúlveda family. Had Domínguez been able to forsee this, it is doubtful that he would have behaved differently. Accumulating an astonishing number of debts while enjoying the amusements of the nearby Pueblo, he gave little attention to the Rancho and did practically nothing to develop its potential.

It was not until 1800, when he was approaching sixty-five and losing his eyesight, that Domínguez finally came to reside permanently at the Rancho. By then, it was too late for him to take an active part in its management. Five years later, totally blind, he once again left to spend his last years with his nephew, Cristóbal, in San Juan Capistrano.

While there, he may have, in the way of old men who like to spin tales, told his tiny grand-nephew, Manuel, about the vast rolling land, stretching to the shining sea, that one day would be his. In any event, it was little Manuel who, twenty years later, was to take over the Rancho San Pedro and make it into one of the most successful ranchos in Southern California.

When Domínguez died, in 1809, he was past seventy-two. He had lived a full life, had seen distinguished military service, but had been incapable of making an adequate adjustment to civilian responsibilities. In his will, he made no specific mention of the Rancho but left one-half of his property to his nephew, Cristóbal, and the other half to the three children of his foreman and good friend Mateo Rubio. He named as executor of his will, Manuel Gutiérrez, and it was this man who now undertook complete control and management of the Rancho for the next twenty years.

Just exactly what the relationship was between Domínguez and Gutiérrez is not clear, but apparently they knew each other very well. About twenty years younger than Domínguez, Gutiérrez was also a bachelor, who enjoyed a good time and apparently did not lack for ample funds.

Born in Spain of a prominent family, he came to California from Mexico in 1800.

Soon the tall, handsome Spanish don, well educated, highly talented, and possessed of boundless energy and a pleasing personality, made quite a reputation for himself in the Pueblo of Los Angeles. When Domínguez died, Gutiérrez paid off all Domínguez's debts, moved to the Rancho and assumed full rights of ownership. At this time, Cristóbal Domínguez did nothing to establish his claim. Appalled by his late uncle's debts, which he had no money to pay, and unable to leave his military duties in San Juan Capistrano, he ignored Gutiérrez's activities.

Since Gutiérrez was a shrewd businessman, it was not long before he had put the Rancho on a profitable basis. Within ten years he built the size of its herds to over nine thousand head. Everyone took it for granted that he was the owner of the tract. And it was so listed in the official records of the Pueblo of Los Angeles.

In addition to his successful management of the Rancho, Gutiérrez was active in political affairs. For almost eighteen years, he held the post of Judge of the Plains, in which capacity he supervised the annual cattle roundups and acted as referee in disputes over ownership of stock. In 1811, he was elected to the *Ayuntamiento,* or City Council, of Los Angeles, which was considered to be quite a plum for anyone not a resident of the Pueblo proper. Finally, in 1822, he culminated his career by becoming Mayor (*Alcalde*) of Los Angeles. Unquestionably, these offices added greatly to his power and prestige.

While these events were taking place, during the years 1784 to 1810, little is known about what was happening to the Sepúlvedas. After their participation in the founding of the Pueblo of Los Angeles, the thread of their story is temporarily obscured. But clues provided by the mission records of San Juan Capistrano, San Diego, and San Gabriel indicate that they must have moved about quite a bit.

Juan José Sepúlveda, the boy who was seventeen when his family arrived on the dusty site of the Pueblo of Los Angeles, was married in San Juan Capistrano on January 10, 1786. His wife's name was Tomasa Gutiérrez. Whether she was related to the prominent Manuel of the Rancho San Pedro is not known. On March 25, 1793, she gave birth to José Dolores Sepúlveda, the future owner of the Rancho de los Palos Verdes. Both she and her husband, Juan José, died before José Dolores had reached the age of sixteen.

The young José must have been both brave and enterprising. If his mother was actually related to Manuel Gutiérrez, it would have been easier for him to approach the great man. But, whether or not this was the case, it is known that by 1810 he had obtained Gutiérrez's permission to run cattle on that part of the Rancho San Pedro that was to become his. Thus was established all future claims of the Sepúlvedas.

Quite an impressive feat for a seventeen-year-old boy!

There was no reason to think that Gutiérrez didn't have the right to do as he wished with the land. It was assumed that the Domínguez heirs had abandoned the tract. So the young Dolores settled down to develop his property. By astute management he was able to increase the size of his stock, and there is some evidence that he even made a payment to Gutiérrez to further strengthen his claim to the land of los Palos Verdes.

Then, like a bolt from the blue, came the news that Cristóbal Domínguez had laid claim to the property that had belonged to his uncle!

Domínguez petitioned Governor Sola, protesting the occupation of "unauthorized parties" of the Rancho San Pedro, and specifically requesting "that Dolores Sepúlveda withdraw the cattle which he had on the Rancho, as the latter by no means possesses a right to keep stock" there. In 1817, the Governor issued a terse decree, stating that the Rancho belonged to Domínguez and ordering Sepúlveda to vacate.

Fortunately, it was only necessary at this point for Sepúlveda to stand his ground and refuse to abandon his home, as Cristóbal Domínguez did nothing to press his advantage. For unknown reasons, he took no further action for five years. Then, in 1822, when Mexico declared its independence from Spain, he once again bestirred himself.

In the closing months of Sola's terms, he requested a personal interview with the Governor and called attention to the decree of 1817. He then managed to obtain a second decree assigning the land to him and was instructed to present the document personally to the *Ayuntamiento* of Los Angeles.

Past sixty, and in very poor health, Cristóbal Domínguez sent his son, Manuel, on his behalf. The young Domínguez was intelligent and aggressive. He capably presented the decree and consulted with Pueblo officials about the removal of Dolores Sepúlveda and other unauthorized occupants. Ironically, Manuel Gutiérrez was at this time Mayor of Los Angeles. Because he was most obviously an interested party, the *Ayuntamiento* directed him to delegate enforcement of the decree to other municipal officals.

When José Dolores Sepúlveda was served notice by officials of the *Ayuntamiento* that he must vacate los Palos Verdes, he flatly refused to comply.

The notion of abandoning all that he had worked to build up was unthinkable. By this time, he had enlarged his home, made substantial improvements on the property, and his cattle numbered well over eight hundred head. Also, he had to provide for a growing family: four sons, Ygnacio and Diego in addition to Juan and José Loreto, and four-month-old Teresa.

He took immediate action to fight for his land. He filed a formal counter-claim with the Pueblo officials, insisting that he was entitled to remain "by original permission from Manuel Gutiérrez and by reason of having made substantial improvements during a long period of residence on the tract." Then he took off for Monterey to make a personal appeal to the new Mexican Governor, Luis Argüello.

On his way back he stopped overnight at the Mission de la Purísima Concepción, north of Santa Barbara. There the tragedy occurred that ended his life. During the night there was a revolt of the Indian neophytes and one of their arrows killed him.

It was now up to Juan and José Loreto to continue the fight which their father had so valiantly fought. But they were only nine and ten years old. Very likely the few personal possessions of José Dolores, which a document in the Los Angeles archives shows as having been turned over to them at this time, had more meaning for them than the Rancho de los Palos Verdes.

Among the articles listed were:

Two coats of first class broadcloth with 35 silver buttons. A decorated saber of silver, edge chipped, harnass destroyed, decorated sheath, with three pieces broken. A good shot gun, with wooden rod. A pair of silver buckles for good spurs.

For the period immediately following Dolores' death Manuel Gutiérrez took over supervision of the Sepúlveda stock. Soon, Doña Sepúlveda remarried, becoming the wife of Antonio Machado, and the family continued to live on the Rancho. Another petition was filed requesting a provisional grant of the land, but nothing came of it. During the ensuing months, the controversy was dormant.

Then on January 6, 1825, an event took place which started a new act in the drama. Cristóbal Domínguez, the veteran soldier, died. And, in the spring, Manuel moved north to take possession of his inheritance.

With him were his mother, the widow of Cristóbal, and his four brothers and sisters. Only a medium-sized pack train was required to transport their unpretentious possessions. The family had only about one hundred dollars to their name, and their stock of cattle was so small that it was no problem for Manuel and his teenage brothers, Nasario and Pedro, to handle them without the aid of hired vaqueros.

For about a year after their arrival, Doña María and her daughters lived in the Pueblo of Los Angeles, as the crude, two-room adobe built by Juan Domínguez was too small to house the whole family. The boys camped there, however, and immediately started developing the property. Manuel assumed complete responsibility.

At twenty-two, he had already commanded respect and admiration. Handsome and outgoing, he made friends easily. It was not long before he was well known in the Pueblo and able to enlist support for his cause.

Soon he had construction well under way on what was to be the permanent home of the Domínguezes, on the northeast slope of the hill which still bears their name. At the start, it was a simple adobe structure, consisting of five rooms. It was to this house that he brought his bride, María Engracia de Cota, whom he married on December 7, 1827. She was one of the loveliest señoritas in all of California and the granddaughter of Manuel Nieto, whose enormous land grant, Los Nietos, bordered the Rancho San Pedro on the southeast.

During this period, Manuel vigorously pursued his contest for ownership of the land. He obtained two decrees from Governor Echeandía for removal of the cattle herds of both the Sepúlvedas and Antonio Machado. But at the same time, Echeandía, who was notorious for his incompetence in the administration of land grants, issued a provisional grant of the Rancho de los Palos Verdes to the Sepúlvedas! Small wonder that Manuel Domínguez was driven to distraction.

In addition, there was the problem of how to enforce the Governor's decrees. Although the Sepúlveda heirs were still only teenage boys, their stepfather, Machado, and their good friend, Gutiérrez, were able to put up an effective fight. When five men were sent out from the Pueblo to help Domínguez in accomplishing the ouster, they were met by a superior force, mobilized for resistance, and plaintively reported back they had been "laughed at."

But Manuel Domínguez was not inclined to start an open fight. He had been married only a few months and was busy getting settled in his new home. The officials at the Pueblo made no further move to resolve the controversy. And so an uneasy truce obtained for about six years.

Meanwhile Juan and José Loreta Sepúlveda were growing up. Despite some hardships, their boyhood years were happy ones. When the ranch work was done, they could roam at will over the Palos Verdes hills and along the Peninsula's rocky shoreline.

Over the brow of San Pedro Hill, a broad canyon trail led down to Portuguese Bend, where there was always the possibility of coming upon some of the sleek, brown animals for whose fur a handsome price could be gotten. Sea otter abounded along the California coast, and it was common practice for Yankee trading vessels to anchor off a lonely stretch of shore and pick up a package of the precious skins.

Everyone participated in the sport and profit of smuggling, with little fear of detection and no sense of dishonor. Quite likely, many a night, in the dark of the moon, the boys would huddle in one of the caves, carved in the cliffs of the Bend, and watch for a boat to steal into the little harbor. Then, quickly, the costly cargo would be exchanged for silver dollars and the boat disappear into the darkness.

It was great fun, too, to ride over the terraced hills, gun ready-at-hand, hunting the myriad wildlife hidden among the tall stalks of mustard. Any day's hunt could bring a covey of quail, a bounding jack rabbit, a fox or coyote, or even a wildcat. And, of course, wandering over the mudflats and sandbars of San Pedro Bay was a never ending source of excitement.

There, on Christmas morning in 1830, Juan and José made a thrilling discovery. It was the wreck of the *Danube,* a brig driven ashore during the night by a fierce southeaster. Then, for many months, they watched a schooner being built with iron and timber from the shipwreck.

This was the first shipbuilding venture in California and the focus of everyone's attention. Sections of the sixty-ton vessel were constructed in the workshops of San Gabriel Mission and transported in ox-drawn carretas to the harbor. Throngs of sidewalk superintendents observed Indians, under the direction of Joseph Chapman, the "regenerated pirate" adopted as man-of-all-work by the Mission fathers, put the pieces together with salvage from the *Danube.* When the schooner, or *goleta,* was finished, Juan and José were part of the great crowd assembled for the launching and accompanying celebration. This took place at Point Goleta, from which today the Vincent Thomas Bridge soars across the Channel.

Occasions such as these, although only a small part of the everyday life of the Rancho, added to its zest and excitement. The boys developed a deep love for the land where they had been born. It was a good life and a wonderful place to be. They were not about to give it up. So, in 1834, when Juan was twenty and José nineteen, they decided to do something to secure their inheritance.

Abalone Cove and Portuguese Point. *(Photo by William Webb)*

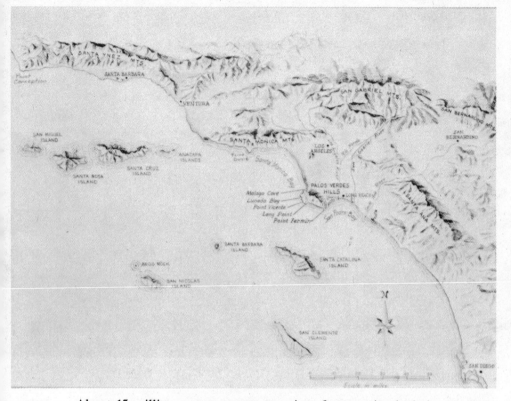

About 15 million years ago, a great rim of mountains had risen to form
a bastion around a huge arm of the sea; this emerging rim is partially
represented today by the Santa Ana, the San Gabriel, and the Santa
Monica Mountains, as well as by the Channel Islands. *(Jack Moffett)*

Harry Phillips, Jr., 1915. The Phillips family raised barley for hay
and grain, transforming the once barren land of the Palos Verdes Peninsula.
Harry Phillips, Sr. was ranch manager for George Bixby.
(Courtesy Palos Verdes Library District, Local History Room)

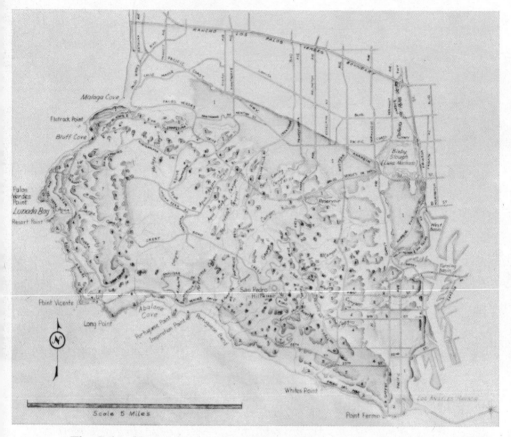

The Palos Verdes Peninsula, showing Points, Coves, Canyons and terrace elevations. *(Jack Moffett)*

The "city" of Rolling Hills; three square miles of country estates, completely enclosed by white rail fencing and entered only through guarded gates.
(Photo by William Webb)

Wayfarer's Chapel.
(Photo by William Webb)

The fountain in the center of the Palos Verdes Plaza is an exact replica of La Fontana del Nettuno in Bologna, Italy. *(Photo by William Webb)*

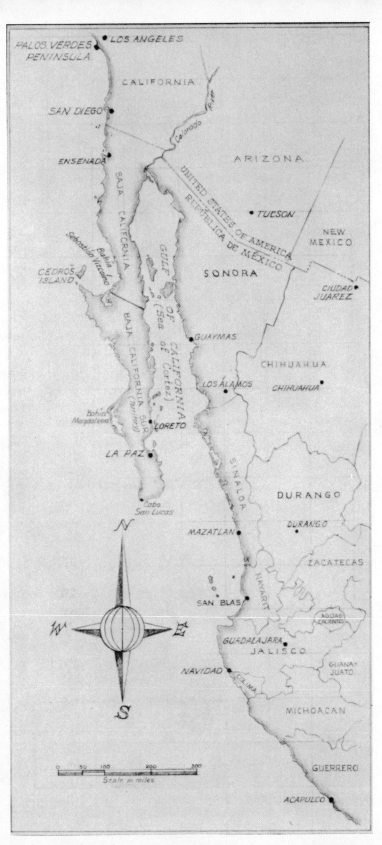

On June 27, 1542, Juan Rodríguez Cabrillo sailed north from Navidad on the expedition that brought him to the shores of the Palos Verdes Peninsula. More than 200 years later a small company of volunteers embarked on a journey from Los Alamos that culminated in the founding of the Pueblo of Los Angeles. Among them was Francisco Xavier Sepúlveda, grandfather of the founder of the Rancho de los Palos Verdes. *(Photo by Jack Moffett)*

Don Abel
Stearns.
*(Courtesy of the
Seaver Center for
Western History
Research, Natural
History Museum
of Los Angeles
County)*

Commodore
Robert F. Stockton.
*(Courtesy of the Seaver
Center for Western
History Research, Natural
History Museum of Los
Angeles County)*

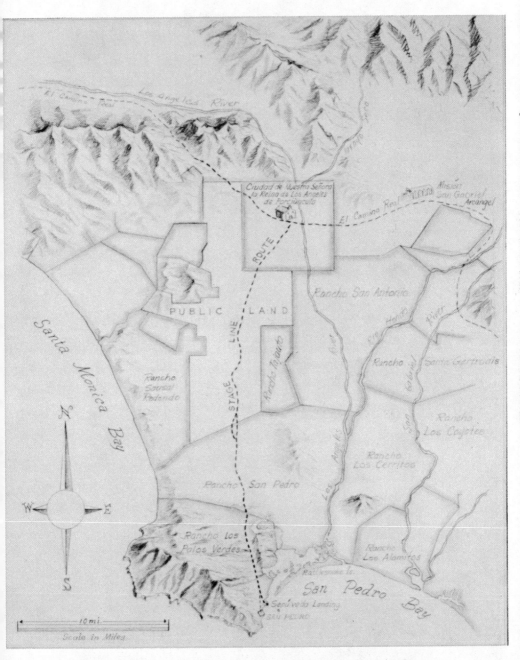

The Rancho de los Palos Verdes, with neighboring ranchos and stage line to the Ciudad of Los Angeles, in the 1850s. *(Jack Moffett)*

Home of Don Diego Sepúlveda
(Courtesy of Everett G. Hager

José Sepúlveda,
Alcalde of Los Angeles.
*(Courtesy of the Seaver Center
for Western History Research,
Natural History Museum of
Los Angeles County)*

Phineas Banning.
(Reproduction by permission of The Huntington Library, San Marino, California)

Home of Phineas Banning.
(Courtesy of the Seaver Center for Western History Research, Natural History Museum of Los Angeles County)

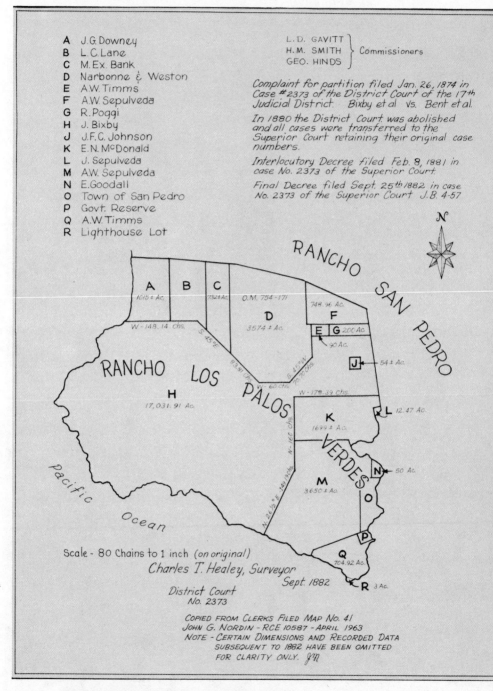

Partition Map of the Rancho Los Palos Verdes, September 25, 1882. *(Courtesy of John G. Nordin)*

With the help of Manuel Gutiérrez, that venerable old gentleman who had so long been their patron, they approached Manuel Domínguez and suggested that the entire case concerning the Rancho be submitted for settlement to the new Governor, José Figueroa. Domínguez was willing to do so, being equally anxious to bring the matter to a head and hoping to have it settled in his favor. A hearing was petitioned and the four claimants, Domínguez, Gutiérrez, and the Sepúlveda brothers journeyed to Monterey to appeal to the Governor.

The hearing was dramatic.

First, a tall, distinguished-looking gentleman, with snow white hair and piercing eyes, rose to present his case. Calmly and deliberately, Manuel Gutiérrez addressed Governor Figueroa.

Willingly he had paid the debts of his old friend. Believing that Domínguez would have wanted him to do so, he had undertaken full responsibility for the Rancho. And as Cristóbal Domínguez had pressed no claim, he had presumed the land belonged to him.

When Manuel Gutiérrez sat down, the Governor nodded gravely to Manuel Domínguez. The handsome, young man stepped forward with grace and assurance. In soft, persuasive tones, he started to speak.

His claim to the Rancho was based on law. Had not Governor Sola twice issued decrees stating that the Rancho belonged to the Domínguez heirs? Had not Governor Echeandía ordered that the land be vacated by those who had no right to be there? Had not the officials of the *Ayuntamiento* of Los Angeles served notice that the Sepúlvedas must leave los Palos Verdes? Surely it was time for justice to be done.

Governor Figueroa turned to Juan and José Sepúlveda. José gave his brother a quick, warm smile of encouragement. Then Juan leaped to his feet. In a voice choked with emotion, he pled for the land that he loved.

Manuel Gutiérrez had given his father permission to occupy los Palos Verdes at a time when Gutiérrez was considered to be the owner of the Rancho San Pedro. Dolores Sepúlveda had taken possession of the property in good faith. It was seven years before Cristóbal Domínguez had taken any action to establish a claim. Meanwhile his father had stocked the land with cattle and worked hard to give life to a tract which had been absolutely deserted.

Justice demanded that the heirs of Dolores Sepúlveda not be denied their birthright!

When Juan was finished, the hearing adjourned until the following day. Manuel Domínguez left the room alone. Gutiérrez walked out with his arms around the young Sepúlvedas. But his eyes as they followed the proud figure of Manuel were filled with sorrow.

The group reconvened in the morning. Suspense mounted as they waited for the Governor to speak. Anxiously they strained forward as he shuffled through the papers on his desk. Finally, he gave his decision.

The entire Palos Verdes area was awarded to the Sepúlvedas!

Juan and José could not contain their joy. Hugging one another ecstatically, they hardly heard the Governor's concluding words. Gutiérrez was to be permitted to pasture his cattle on the Rancho for the remainder of his life, but he was not to have any rights of ownership to the land.

The slow smile which came over the seventy-five-year-old gentleman's face clearly indicated that he was well satisfied with the decision. Having no heirs of his own, he was happy for the Sepúlvedas. Then, his glance darted to Manuel Domínguez.

A dark flush discolored the young man's handsome features. He held himself under rigid control until the Governor dismissed the group, then bolted from the room. The fact that the rest of the Rancho was unconditionally his did not appease his anger.

The Arbitration Decree of 1834 marked the beginning of a prosperous period for the Sepúlvedas. Although the land controversy continued to smolder for the next twelve years, periodically erupting into fresh litigation, it was pushed into the background. Flourishing in an unaccustomed sense of security, Juan and José both married and began to create new lives for themselves.

Juan built a home on a hill near the present intersection of Gaffey Street and Anaheim Boulevard, overlooking Machado Lake. José's house was farther south, on the west side of the dusty lane that became Gaffey Street. The sites were well chosen, with ample water and welcome shade provided by tall sycamores and alders.

The houses were very simply built, with adobe walls, wide window sills, and dirt floors. There were only three rooms: kitchen, combination living and dining room, and bedroom. The roof was covered with asphaltum, plentiful on the Peninsula, and braziers filled with glowing charcoal provided the heating. In the center of the patio was a well for the water supply.

This type of dwelling was customary for young couples of modest means. As the finances of the family improved and its size increased, additional rooms were added, until a substantial establishment completely encircled the patio. Also, as there was more money to spend, more elaborate furnishings were obtained and the earthen floors covered with tile or fashionable wide planks of wood.

When the brides of Juan and José, the lovely Felipa and Cesaria, shopped for furniture, they were happy to get plain wooden tables and benches and a couple of Mission chairs. A tiny Spanish butterfly table was considered a great luxury. Their beds consisted of rude frames and strands of rawhide strung across to support the mattresses. Dishes were of bright, sturdy Talavera pottery made in Mexico.

Trees and shrubs, transplanted from the San Gabriel Mission, lent charm to their patio gardens. A fig tree and a pomegranate stood near the well, and grapevines covered the *corredor*. The sweet perfume of jasmine and roses wafted through the windows. Life was peaceful and pastoral.

Cattle raising was the chief interest of Juan and José. Their ever-increasing herds roamed the vast open spaces of the Palos Verdes Peninsula. Although no fences separated the Rancho de los Palos Verdes from neighboring ranchos, they were not concerned. Each man had his registered brand, and, at regularly held rodeos, the herds were segregated and the interests of the owners protected by the Judge of the Plains.

A jaunt into Los Angeles was always a welcome diversion. Its status now changed from *Pueblo* (village) to *Ciudad* (city), it was the hub of a population of over fifteen hundred white men, women, and children, and over five hundred domesticated Indians. The jurisdiction of the city extended from San Juan Capistrano to Santa Barbara, and from San Bernardino to the Pacific Ocean.

By 1835, Los Angeles was the largest settlement in California and growing fast. That rivalry between Northern and Southern California had already started was demonstrated by the refusal of Monterey officials to recognize an official decree naming Los Angeles as capital of California. Ten years passed before they moved there.

Around the Plaza, dominated by the church, was a large community of houses, shops, and places of amusement. From it radiated in all directions the dusty trails over which the rancheros galloped into town. When Juan and José rode in to arrange a cattle deal, or to see about a new saddle, they came along a route roughly paralleling the present-day Harbor Freeway.

Dressed for the occasion in broad-brimmed hats, jackets of bright colored cloth, flaring pantaloons slit below the knees, with red sashes wound around their waists and brilliant serapes draped over their shoulders, they were a dashing pair. While in the city, they usually found time for a game of monte, or took in a horse race or a bullfight. Sometimes they stopped to chat with Nathaniel Pryor, who was to marry their sister, Teresa. But always, long before the sun dipped toward the western sky, they headed through the sea of tall mustard stalks to the distant mound of the Palos Verdes Hills.

Felipa and Cesaria Sepúlveda also journeyed into the *Ciudad,* but much less frequently than their husbands. For them, it was a long, hard trip in an ox-drawn carreta, taking almost from sunrise to sundown. Cushioned with pillows, the carretas were built of rawhide, with sections of logs for wheels that squeaked horribly even when doused with oil. An Indian servant walked beside the cart, prodding the oxen with a long goad to keep them moving. But despite their discomforts, they made a charming picture in jewel-colored dresses and silver-buckled shoes, their shining hair piled high on splendid combs, and gold necklaces and earrings glinting against their long black mantillas.

Usually they stayed for a couple of nights with the Lugos or the Carrillos, while they shopped the city. Juan Temple had a large, general merchandise store on Main Street, as did Abel Stearns. These were fascinating places, offering everything from New England hardware to Chinese shawls. The Señoras Sepúlveda would have had a great deal of difficulty leaving them had they not had veritable "floating department stores" off the shores of their own property.

By this time, San Pedro had become the most important port on the Pacific Coast. Although inhospitable as a harbor, and bleak and unpretentious in appearance, it was the mecca of trading vessels from all over the world, and this in complete defiance of first Spanish and then Mexican law. It also became a favorite smuggling center, as there were no local authorities in the area and, for that matter, no residents of any kind. The nearest dwelling was that of José Loreto Sepúlveda.

Because of shallow waters and sandbars, merchant ships had to ride anchor a mile or so offshore. Then, small boats transported cargos and passengers from ship to shore. Often these capsized, spilling both people and goods into the muddy water. This only added to the discomfort of those who had to take the long, dusty ride back to Los Angeles in wet clothing. But no hardship could deter anyone, who could possibly get there, from coming down to San Pedro as soon as he heard that a ship had anchored. And all of them tried to get on board.

The young Sepúlvedas were host to large numbers of strangers, as well as friends and acquaintances, as the road to San Pedro practically went past their front doors. They kept a band of horses for the purpose of transporting those who were not afraid to ride the half-broken broncos. They also built a crude dock and landing at the base of the cliffs in the vicinity of what are now Fourteenth and Beacon Streets in San Pedro. This came to be known as Sepúlveda Landing. Later, when carriages were available, they started a stagecoach line between Los Angeles and the Harbor.

On those days when the ships were in, splendidly dressed rancheros on horseback, brown-robed padres on mules, humble citizens on foot, and creaking carretas piled high with hides or loaded down with excited women and children clogged the narrow road from Los Angeles. Two or more oxen, yoked together by their horns, drew the freight carretas, and the charge for hauling merchandise was twenty dollars a ton. When they finally reached San Pedro, everyone hurried down the steep embankment to the shore, slipping and sliding in their eagerness to get a place on one of the small boats that would take them out to the trading vessels.

On the beach, those who were physically unable to get to the ships sat around bonfires, waiting until well after dark for their turn to trade. During the long, exciting day, Indians stood guard over the oxcarts, while sailors, huge bundles of hides on their heads, plunged through the waves to the large launches waiting beyond the big combers.

Those who did reach the vessels were rewarded with a dazzling array of wondrous things: exquisitely embroidered shawls, jewel boxes and housewares, candlesticks and watches, sugar and spices, satins and silks, and even an occasional rosewood piano. It was a veritable fairyland for both young and old. And the banknotes used to buy the tantalizing array of merchandise were hides, worth two dollars each.

All year round, the enormous trade in hides and tallow continued. A published report states that in the single year of 1834, from one hundred to one hundred and twenty thousand hides and twenty-five hundred quintals of tallow were exported from the port. In order to facilitate the trade, a small adobe warehouse, one hundred feet long and forty feet wide, was built on the site now occupied by Fort MacArthur.

Originally constructed by the San Gabriel Mission fathers, it was purchased by Abel Stearns. He used it to great advantage by buying hides and tallow at the convenience of the rancheros and storing them there so that they could be sold to Yankee merchants whenever their ships came into the harbor. Teresa Sepúlveda's fiancée, Nathaniel Pryor, worked for Stearns and, in this way, built up enough capital eventually to purchase all the property along what is now Alameda Street between First and Aliso.

Much of the feeling of the southeast end of the Palos Verdes Peninsula, especially during the stormy months of winter, has been captured by Richard Henry Dana, in his celebrated book, *Two Years Before the Mast:*

"The land was of a clayey quality, and, as far as the eye could see bare of trees and even shrubs; and there was no sign of a town—not even a house . . . No sooner had we come to anchor, than the slip-rope, and the other preparations for southeasters, were got ready; and there was reason enough for it, for we lay exposed to every wind that could blow . . . As soon as everything was snug on board, the boat was lowered and we pulled ashore . . . As we drew in we found the tide low, and the rocks and stones, covered with kelp and seaweed, lying bare for the distance of an eighth of a mile. Leaving the boat, and picking our way barefoot over these, we came to what is called the landing-place at high-water mark . . . Just in front of the landing, and immediately over it, was a small hill . . . not more than thirty or forty feet high . . . . Going up . . . we saw close behind it a small low building with one room, containing a fireplace, cooking apparatus, and the rest of it unfinished and used to store goods. The nearest house was a rancho, or cattle farm, about three miles off . . .

"The next day (our agent) went up to visit the Pueblo and the neighboring missions; and in a few days . . . large ox-carts and droves of mules, loaded with hides, were seen coming over the flat country. We loaded our long-boat with goods of all kinds . . . and pulled ashore. After landing and rolling them over the stones upon the beach, we stopped, waiting for the carts to come down the hill and take them; but the captain soon settled the matter by ordering us to carry them all up to the top . . . The hill was low, but steep, and the earth, being clayey and wet with the recent rains, was but bad holding-ground for our feet. The heavy barrels and casks we rolled up with some difficulty, getting behind and putting our shoulders to them; now and then our feet slipping, adding to the danger of the casks rolling back upon us. But the greatest trouble was with the large boxes of sugar. These we had to place upon oars, and lifting them up, rest the oars upon our shoulders, and creep slowly up the hill with the gait of a funeral procession. After an hour or so of hard work, we got them all up, and found the carts standing full of hides, which we had to unload, and to load the carts again with our goods . . .

"Now the hides were to be got down; and for this purpose we brought the boat around to a place where the hill was steeper, and threw them off, letting them slide over the slope. Many of them lodged, and we had to let ourselves down and set them going again, and in this way became covered with dust, and our clothes torn. After we had the hides all down, we were obliged to take them on our heads, and walk over the stones and through the water to the boat. The water and the stones together would wear out a pair of shoes a day, and as shoes were very scarce and very dear, we were compelled to go barefooted. At night we went on board, having had the hardest and most disagreeable day's work that we had yet experienced.''

Today it is still possible to go down the steep cliffs at Point Fermin, over which Dana and his companions pitched armloads of hides, and walk about on the sharp, slippery stones. The cattle farm to which he referred was, of course, the Rancho de los Palos Verdes, and the horse obtained to transport the ship's agent to Los Angeles was one from the Sepúlveda *caballada,* kept in readiness near the home of José Loreto.

From Dana's point of view, the Peninsula appeared drab and barren, and small wonder considering the conditions under which he worked. He could hardly have been expected to appreciate its wild, desolate beauty, or to see the silvery sage, bright green cactus, or tall yellow mustard as anything but impediments to progress over the rolling hills.

The Sepúlvedas also were little interested in the seaward side of los Palos Verdes. The best grazing land was on the north slopes of the hills and on the adjacent flat country, and their first concern was to increase their herds. Cattle was the chief source of both food and wealth. Beef was the principal dietary staple of the day, and tallow was needed for soap, candles, and cooking fat. The rawhides were used in making reatas, bridle reins, chair bottoms, bedsprings, and even floor mats. In addition, of course, they constituted the basic currency or medium of exchange.

In the 1830s, the Sepúlvedas were just beginning to establish their financial and social positions, and their families were growing. Before the decade was over, Juan would have two children and José Loreto three. It was important for them to cultivate their resources, especially as the smoldering land controversy continued to represent a nagging worry.

Manuel Domínguez had already achieved considerable political power; first as a member of the *Ayuntamiento,* and then as *Alcalde* and representative to the provincial legislature. He could be a most formidable adversary.

Although these were happy and optimistic days for young Juan and José Loreto, they were also a time to shore up and prepare for the future. Turbulent days were ahead not only for them, but for all Californians.

5

A Time of Testing

THE YEAR WAS 1839. It was a lovely June morning, the air soft and sweet, with a light breeze from the harbor wafting in a hint of the sea. The voices of tiny José Dolores and Petra Pilar came from the house where they were playing under the supervision of an old Indian woman, maid-of-all-work in the Sepúlveda household.

Cesaria Sepúlveda sighed contentedly as she walked through the patio to the small *huerta*. Heavy with child, she still bent to work among the fragrant herbs in her kitchen garden. The feel of the earth was good on her fingers, and the warm sunshine soothed the slight ache in her back.

Basking in the pale golden beauty of the day, she couldn't help hoping that her beloved husband would be back before sundown. José Loreto had gone to Los Angeles on business and stayed the night with his sister and brother-in-law, the Pryors. Even for such a short time she missed him.

Thinking of Teresa Pryor, Cesaria frowned. The girl had not been looking at all well lately. She had been only fifteen when she married Nathaniel and barely sixteen when little Pablo was born.

Cesaria shook her head. She really didn't like Nathaniel. He was too rough and aggressive.

Last October, José and Juan had been terribly upset when Nathaniel filed his petition with the Governor asking for four thousand acres along the east side of los Palos Verdes. Everyone knew the land belonged to Manuel Domínguez.

It was an upstart thing for him to do. Of course, he claimed he was doing it for Teresa. But it looked more as if he were using her.

When Governor Alvarado issued a decree, stating in no uncertain terms that there could be no allowance to the petition, as the land was private property, Nathaniel had laughed.

"Well, it was a good try anyway," he said and shrugged his huge shoulders.

But Cesaria knew that José was still worried. It was unfortunate to have added to the bad feeling between the Domínguez and Sepúlveda families.

Cesaria gathered a handful of thyme and oregano and started towards the house. It was time to see about the preparation of the midday meal. Passing the Castilian rose bush, she stopped to pick a few of the lovely pink blossoms for the small household altar. Then, she heard the thunder of hooves down the road and looked up to see José galloping up the driveway.

Her heart sank when she saw the look on his face.

Slowly and wearily, he dismounted. Approaching her, he said in a voice thickened by grief and anger.

"We're in trouble again." He waved a piece of paper. "Domínguez submitted another petition for our land. And we've been ordered to leave."

So began two years of worry and heartache.

Immediately after being served notice of the Governor's decree of ouster, José and Juan filed a cross complaint citing Governor Figueroa's Arbitration Decree of 1834. As this had declared the land unequivocally theirs, it seemed incredible that the matter was not settled. But time dragged on and no word came.

What made their time of trouble seem particularly dark was that they faced it alone. Their brothers, Diego and Ygnacio, both still bachelors, were off on their own, completely disinterested in the Rancho. In fact, in July of 1840, Ygnacio conveyed his interest in los Palos Verdes to his brother-in-law, Nathaniel Pryor, for fifty dollars in goods, declaring "that it is not worth more, neither did he find anyone that would have given him as much."

Having alienated the Governor by his earlier action, Pryor could be of no help to the Sepúlvedas. Worst of all they were deprived of the support and counsel of their great, good friend, Manuel Gutiérrez, who died in 1839. To add to their sorrow, they lost their beloved sister, Teresa, in September of 1840.

At last, in April of 1841, the Sepúlvedas were summoned before Governor Alvarado. Gratefully, they heard that their claim was once again upheld.

Speaking with great severity, the Governor admonished both Manuel Domínguez and the Sepúlvedas to adhere strictly to the terms of the decree of 1834. He further stipulated that a penalty of one thousand dollars would be assessed for any violation by either party.

Juan and José looked at each other knowingly. They had long suspected that Nathaniel Pryor's rash action had had a great deal to do with bringing this trouble with Manuel Domínguez. Now, they exchanged courtly bows with the tall, distinguished-looking don.

Domínguez nodded gravely, then flashed his warm, disarming smile.

"This must now settle the matter between our families," he said. "We will sign an agreement."

And so, following a survey to determine the proper boundary lines between Rancho San Pedro and Rancho de los Palos Verdes, in June, 1841, an agreement was signed by the Domínguez family transferring all right to los Palos Verdes to the Sepúlvedas. The portion which fell to Juan and José Loreto comprised 31,629.43 acres. The long and bitter battle was over.

As the fortunes of the Sepúlveda family once again became bright and propitious for prosperity, the political scene in Southern California became increasingly turbulent. Throughout the thirties, Mexico's control over and even interest in California had gradually weakened. A series of revolutions and counter-revolutions, with Los Angeles as the center of intrigue, kept California in constant turmoil. No sooner was a governor sent from Mexico than he was overthrown. Finally, the cauldron came to full boil with the arrival of Micheltorena and his ragamuffin army.

At first the Angelenos welcomed the new governor, as they had hopes of persuading him to stay and thus make their city the permanent capital. Ever since 1835, the seat of government had been jumping back and forth between Los Angeles and Monterey, according to the whim of successive governors. Following the administration of his oath of office, on New Year's Eve, 1842, Micheltorena was given a splendid inaugural ball that lasted a full week, with fiestas, fandangos, and bull-and-bear fights.

The Sepúlvedas, along with families from all the surrounding ranchos, came to the city for the brilliant event. They were welcomed at the spacious town house of their cousin, José Andrés Sepúlveda, wealthy owner of the Rancho San Joaquin, which is today known as the Irvine Ranch. Open-handed hospitality was also offered to them at the Ávila house, as their mother was a member of that renowned, old California family.

It was at the Ávila adobe, close by the Plaza, that the family breakfast was interrupted on the second day of the festivities by a hysterical Indian servant who had discovered the vegetable garden ravaged and fruit trees picked bare. This was only one of numerous instances of the raiding activities of Micheltorena's army of thieves and cutthroats. Soon the city was only too glad to get rid of the Governor and his entourage.

Within two years, Micheltorena had outworn his welcome in the north as well. Revolts flared all over California, and in February, 1845, word came that once again the hated Governor was marching south. Angelenos quickly mustered a force of resistance. The battle which ensued, in the vicinity of the present Studio City, was full of noise and mock ferocity but resulted in no bloodshed. When the Americans, who made up a substantial number of participants on both sides of the fracas, hoisted a white flag and opened the parley for peaceful settlement, Micheltorena was defeated.

With characteristic California generosity, he was permitted to keep his arms and march to San Pedro harbor with full military honors. Now the Angelenos had what they wanted. Pío Pico, their own choice and a Southern Californian, was named governor, and Los Angeles was capital. Unfortunately, their triumph was destined to be short-lived. Real war clouds were gathering on the horizon.

During the 1840s, two forces, which were markedly to affect the history of California, were gathering strength. One was the dissatisfaction of native Californians, as well as American settlers, with Mexican rule. The other was an increasing desire on the part of the United States to acquire California. The latter reached its culmination when President Polk, setting the acquisition of California and Texas as the chief goals of his administration, called for outright war.

On the morning of August 6th, 1846, Juan and José Sepúlveda were down at Stearns' warehouse discussing a hide shipment, when a strange ship appeared on the horizon. There was something vaguely familiar about its outline. Then suddenly, Juan remembered. An American Commodore had come on a ship like this, several years ago, and with his retinue had marched into Los Angeles to pay his respects to Governor Micheltorena.

This was an American warship!

The brothers flung themselves on their horses and galloped to the top of San Pedro Hill. From this vantage point they observed the landing of the first military contingent and, to their complete astonishment, the raising of the American flag. Immediately Juan rode down to their corral and dispatched a messenger to Los Angeles. José stayed to watch the amazing spectacle in the harbor.

All day long a seemingly endless stream of men continued to disembark from the ship. They presented a most peculiar appearance, dressed in a motley assortment of ragged garments of varied kind and color, and with no uniformity in their arms and other accoutrements. This hardly looked like an enemy to be feared.

For the next couple of days, the Americans made rather a pathetic show of drilling and preparing themselves for the inland march to Los Angeles. It was obvious, even at some distance, that these were sailors and not soldiers. Some were armed with carbines, others had only pistols and swords or boarding pikes.

To insure their safety, Juan and José took Felipa and Cesaria, with the children, into Los Angeles to stay with relatives. Then, after communicating their intelligence of what was happening at San Pedro to General José Castro, who was in charge of military operations in the south, they returned to the Rancho to await developments.

Shortly after dawn, the next day, a messenger from General Castro thundered up the Sepúlveda house nearest to the harbor, where the Sepúlveda brothers were just finishing their breakfast. Dashing outside, they caught a couple of horses and galloped after the lone figure bearing a white flag of truce. As they approached the harbor, they saw the Americans marching four abreast in what appeared to be a circle around Abel Stearns' warehouse.

Puzzling over this odd military maneuver, they rode up to the Commodore, a stern forbidding man, whom they knew to be Robert Stockton. He was standing beside the mouth of a large carronade, the only exposed part of a group of guns covered with canvas. The huge, gaping aperture by which he had stationed himself added considerably to the grimness of the encounter. But with a bow, and a flourish of his broadbrimmed hat, Castro's messenger presented his dispatch to the Commodore.

Stockton listened stolidly while an interpreter read the message aloud. General Castro ''warned the Commodore to desist from the contemplated expedition and proposed a truce, by the terms of which, each party should maintain his present position, unmolested by the other, until intelligence of a more definite nature could be obtained from Mexico or until conclusion of the peace.''

Drawing himself up to his full height, the Commodore let loose a fierce barrage of words in tones of the most hostile and implacable determination. The content of the speech, as relayed by the interpreter, was equally offensive.

He ''directed the Californians to return to their master and inform him that the American commander intended to march immediately on the Ciudad de Los Angeles . . . General Castro should prepare to surrender his arms, disperse his forces and require his men to return to their homes . . . he would not negotiate with him on any other terms than those of absolute submission to the authority of the United States.''

Then the Commodore added the final insult.

Imperiously, he waved Castro's emissaries from his presence and shouted, ''Vamose!''

Burning with indignation, the men rode away to report to the General. They did not meet with the expected response. Many Angelenos found the prospect of American rule little more hateful than that of Mexico. Some even felt that with the coming of the Americans ''we will have peace and quiet in the land, as in the good old days of the king.'' There is evidence to support the theory that Castro himself was party to a secret plan to declare California independent ''as soon as a sufficient number of foreigners should arrive.''

Nevertheless, full of bombast if not bravery, Castro again dispatched emissaries to Stockton. In boastful and sonorous language, he informed the Commodore ''that in case he advanced his defeat was certain, and that the Californians were determined to the last man to perish in defense of their country.'' This attempt to negotiate received the same reception as had the first.

On August 11th, Stockton began his march to Los Angeles.

While the Americans were advancing over the hot dusty plain, they were harried by a few intrepid Californians who were unwilling to surrender so easily. United States military records show that the ''enemies were often in sight, threatening their flanks or advance ground and hovering on the brows of the adjacent hills.'' Undoubtedly, the Sepúlvedas were among those who did what they could, but they received no support.

Instead, on the 12th, when Stockton's men were only a few miles from the city, Castro sent another courier bearing still another pompous message. "If the Commodore marched upon the town he would find it the grave of his men."

Actually, when the Americans marched into Los Angeles on August 13th, it looked deserted. Without firing a shot, Castro had broken camp, dispersed his army and with a handful of followers fled to Mexico. The next day those officers who had stayed were placed on parole, upon condition that they would not again take up arms against the United States.

The conquest of the Californians appeared to be complete. After two weeks among the apparently peaceable Angelenos, Stockton decided to move on. He left Lieutenant Gillespie in charge of a garrison of fifty recently recruited frontiersmen, and sailed for Monterey. But, unfortunately he did not understand the character of these people who seemed so carefree and indolent.

Gillespie was a very poor choice as commandant. He had no qualifications for the position and in addition was vain, arbitrary and dictatorial. His men were equally unsuited for their task. Inexperienced and cocky, they swaggered about the streets showing their contempt of the Californians.

Soon they touched off rebellion among the youths of the city, who started with simple pranks to annoy Gillespie and ended with an attack on the garrison. Gillespie responded in the worst possible way. He clamped down a set of ridiculous restrictions on the entire city.

There were to be no gatherings in private homes. Two or more persons must not walk together on the streets. Liquor could not be sold without permission. Californians could not gallop through the city. Houses were searched. And the most prominent men in town were arrested and interrogated on the slightest suspicion.

The fiery Angelenos rose up in rebellion against these insults. José María Flores was made commandante general, with José Antonio Carrillo and Andrés Pico, second and third in command. The fact that these men were risking their lives by breaking parole did not deter them.

Riders were sent throughout the countryside to gather guns and ammunition, and all available carretas were pressed into service to transport the arms into Los Angeles. The main camp of the rebels was across the river, on Paredon Blanco, now Boyle Heights. To this place they hauled a small bronze cannon, normally used for ceremonial salutes, which had been buried for safekeeping on the property of a sweet old lady, named Doña Reyes. Later in the war this cannon, nicknamed "the old woman's gun," was to play an important part in routing the second

American invasion across the land of los Palos Verdes.

Now the Californians had Gillespie entirely at their mercy. Short of food and water, he was desperate. On the 24th of September he was visited by a tall lanky American storekeeper named John Brown, who volunteered to ride to Monterey and advise Stockton of conditions in Los Angeles. With a brief message from Gillespie written on cigarette papers concealed in his long hair, "Lean John" stole out of the beleaguered camp in the dead of night and rode away for help.

But Gillespie couldn't wait to be rescued. He was outnumbered by the Californians at least ten to one. When Flores sent a formal demand for surrender, reinforced by a shot from the little bronze cannon, Gillespie capitulated.

The gallant Californians permitted him to evacuate his position unmolested. So, once again, a band of weary men trudged across the long dusty miles to San Pedro, flags flying and drums beating, but thoroughly discouraged and beaten. There they boarded a merchant ship, at anchor in the harbor, and awaited orders.

On October 6th they saw the frigate *Savannah* appear with reinforcements. After covering 600 miles in less than six days, "Lean John" had reached Commodore Stockton, and Captain William Mervine was ordered to sail south. High on the hills of Palos Verdes, Juan and José Sepúlveda watched the Americans begin to disembark.

Instantly Juan, who was in charge of forty-five men on reconnaissance patrol at San Pedro, dispatched a courier to warn Flores. In Los Angeles, the news was received with a frenzied attempt to prepare for the defense. First the daring Carrillo spurred southward with fifty men. Then Flores followed more slowly, bringing the "old woman's gun."

The day was suffocatingly hot with not a breath of air stirring. Clouds of dust rose around the long lines of sailors, marines, and soldiers as they marched along the narrow canyon road between the hills of the Rancho de los Palos Verdes. The Sepúlvedas estimated that there were as many as 400 of them.

A few of them were on horseback, taken from the Sepúlveda corral, the rest on foot, and they had no cannon. Juan led a few forays, trying to harry the enemy as much as possible, but his orders were to remain with his contingent at San Pedro, which he did.

By midafternoon the Americans had advanced as far as the Domínguez hacienda, where they made camp. Carrillo and his advance guard were on the scene. Their force was not sufficiently strong to attack the enemy; nevertheless, withdrawing to a strategic position in a nearby canyon, they kept up enough intermittent fire to harrass them.

Then at midnight Flores arrived with the little cannon, clumsily bound to a couple of carreta wheels. He ordered Carrillo's men to assume battle formation and the "old woman's gun" was wheeled into place on a prominence facing the hacienda. Towards morning a young artillery officer, Ygnacio Aguilar, was ordered to fire the cannon. With considerable difficulty because of the awkward way the gun was mounted, he finally managed to fire a ball which, striking one of the porch posts, knocked part of the roof away and showered debris.

The Americans came tumbling out of the house in disarray. Hastily they lined up in formation and started their march towards Los Angeles. To confuse them Carrillo cleverly ordered his men to make a detour and, when their swift horses had placed them well ahead of the enemy, lie in ambush on both sides of the road with the cannon placed athwart the enemy's line of march.

Instantly, the mounted Californians pulled the gun out of reach with their long reatas. Again and again the cannon was loaded and fired; each time it fell short of its mark but was saved from enemy capture by the quick action of the Californians. Soon their small supply of cannonballs was exhausted. Fearlessly, they galloped in among the Americans and retrieved the precious ammunition.

At last, someone produced a small cache of gunpowder of a better quality but sufficient for only one or two shots. Carefully Aguilar aimed at the advancing Americans. The little cannon roared and this time it had a devastating effect, blasting through the enemy column and killing or wounding several men.

The Americans fell back in confusion. When order was restored in their ranks they beat a hasty retreat. Exhausted from the intense heat and the exertion of battle, footsore and weary, they carried their dead and wounded as best they could. The Californians disdained to harass them further, satisfied to have gained control of the battlefield without wounding a single one of their men.

From the Sepúlveda house, which the brothers had made into a secure fortification, Juan and José saw the Americans come trudging across the plain. Jubilant at this evidence of victory, Juan mobilized his men to do their part. He ordered them to lie in ambush above the road, and as the enemy passed they fired several rounds of shot into their lines.

The same evening about eight o'clock, a contingent of thirty men appeared, sent by Flores, to take over Juan's post and bearing orders for Juan to move his troops to San Pedro and there maintain observation of the enemy's movements. He did so and, as night fell, saw the Americans hastening aboard their ship, the *Savannah*.

The next morning he observed several small boats making their way from the ship to El Morro Island (later called Dead Man's Island). About fifty men landed. Some of them set about digging a huge hole while others mounted a small piece of artillery on the highest point of the island and proceeded to fire at the mainland.

Their shots did no damage. Soon it became obvious that the business of the Americans on the island was to bury their dead and the shooting was merely a defensive maneuver. Later in the afternoon, having finished their grim task, they returned to their ship.

For two weeks the *Savannah* lay at anchor. There were no indications of plans to attack. During this time Diego Sepúlveda, the youngest of the Sepúlveda brothers, was given command of the garrison at the Sepúlveda house. For many years he had been absent from the Rancho and it was a pleasant, almost relaxed interlude for the family, despite the warship in the harbor.

Then on October 23rd the *Congress* sailed into San Pedro Bay, bringing Commodore Stockton with reinforcements.

At once he commenced a landing operation, not only of his own men, but also of the troops on the *Savannah*. As they approached the shore, Juan Sepúlveda ordered a brisk fire, but short of ammunition and faced by an overwhelming force, he had to retreat. Immediately he dispatched a courier to alert Flores and Carrillo.

The enemy, made cautious by the recent encounter with the Californians, remained on the beach at San Pedro for several days. Carrillo used the time to advantage, devising a remarkable defense.

First he deployed his cavalry among the hills and ravines of Palos Verdes. Then he ordered them to ride single file in a circle, repeatedly passing through a gap in the hills in such a way that they appeared to the enemy as three times their actual number. Stockton had used this same technique in his first invasion of San Pedro, but he didn't recognize it.

In addition, Carrillo had his horsemen attach pieces of brush, hides and other objects to reatas and drag them along the ground, raising clouds of dust through which other horsemen dashed in and out. Partially obscured from the enemy's view, they looked like a tremendous force. Stockton assumed their number to be at least 800 and panicked.

By ten o'clock that night, boats from both warships came ashore, and with much haste and confusion the Americans took flight. Within a few days of his return to San Pedro, Stockton sailed for San Diego, defeated by the courage and ingenuity of the Californians.

Great was the rejoicing for the next few days, both in the city and on the Rancho de los Palos Verdes. But the war wasn't over. An American army under the command of Colonel Stephen Kearny was marching across the continent to the coast.

At this critical moment events in Los Angeles destroyed the Californians' hard-earned advantage. Petty jealousy, hot temper and intrigue resulted in a rift between Flores and Carrillo. Shooting broke out in the streets and in the confusion Flores' horses stampeded out of town. Two days later an uneasy peace found the Angelenos badly split by dissension.

Then suddenly a frantic plea for help came from Andrés Pico. He had encountered Kearny's forces at San Pasqual, in the mountains between San Diego and the Warner's Ranch, and dealt them a stunning blow. He needed reinforcements to finish off the crippled American army which was making its way to San Diego. Flores, with rebellion in his own ranks, could do nothing.

Kearny succeeded in reaching Stockton in San Diego, and on December 29th their combined troops, numbering some 600 men, marched up the coast to Los Angeles. Simultaneously, Lieutenant Colonel John C. Frémont started down from Monterey with a crew of about 400 soldiers, trappers and settlers. Now Flores was desperate.

Short of ammunition, his army weakened by desertions, he marshaled his forces for a last stand. On the heights overlooking the San Gabriel River, near the present city of Montebello, he assembled what remained of his once-proud cavalry. One of his horsemen was Ygnacio Sepúlveda.

On the morning of January 9, 1847, a bloody engagement took place. Dragging their guns, wallowing in water knee-deep, the Americans tried to force their way across the river. Ygnacio, headstrong and impetuous, led a charge against the struggling column. They were driven back by musket fire. Undaunted, Sepúlveda once again gave the cry to battle.

Alone, he dashed into the riverbed and attempted to scale the precipitous opposite bank. By this time his comrades were at his heels, lances glinting in the sun while enemy guns roared out a deadly volley. In utter confusion, the Californians fell back. Several were wounded. Ygnacio was killed.

Side by side, Kearny and Stockton led the American charges across the river and up the embankment. Briefly the Californians tried to hold their ground but soon gave way. Within a matter of minutes they took flight and San Gabriel Valley resounded to the jubilant shouts of the victorious Americans.

The next morning the triumphant American army again marched into Los Angeles, band playing and flags waving. Except for a few hot-headed youths catcalling from the hill above the Plaza, the city appeared deserted. Houses were bolted and barred against the invaders.

Along with many other residents, Doña Ávila had fled her home. A young boy was left to look after her things with strict instructions to keep doors and windows secured. But the music of the band was too much for him. First he opened the window and peeked out. Then he ran outside to see what was going on. Stockton's men noticed the open house and promptly commandeered it for their temporary headquarters.

On January 11th, Frémont and his buckskin battalion reached San Fernando Valley. By this time the Californians had lost heart. Flores had run away to Mexico, and Pico and Carrillo feared the consequences of their broken parole. When they found that Frémont was amicably disposed towards them, they were quite willing to make peace. On the 13th of January, in the Cahuenga ranch house, Andrés Pico surrendered his sword, ending California's participation in the Mexican War. Formal cession of California to the United States took place the following year.

For a while, Angelenos continued to shun the invaders. Many families left town for their ranchos; those who had to remain stayed behind barred doors. But soon the funloving, easygoing California temperament took over and the city went back to business and pleasure as usual.

Actually American administration caused few changes. The *Ayuntamiento* kept its functions and the *Alcalde* and other civil officers maintained regular activities. At this time José Sepúlveda was second *Alcalde,* and all three Sepúlveda brothers were active in civic affiars.

Diego, one of the owners of the Rancho San Bernardino, was the farthest removed from the scene. In 1844, he had deeded his interest in the Rancho de los Palos Verdes to Santiago Johnson in exchange for the San Bernardino property. Now, just getting under way on the career that was to make him one of the wealthiest men in Southern California, he had little interest in los Palos Verdes and left its problems to his brothers.

At the very beginning of hostilities, Juan and José had prudently petitioned Governor Pío Pico for another confirmation of their title. A grant was issued by the Governor on June 3, 1846, and the boundaries of the tract were again surveyed and marked. They had acted wisely, as within a few years all Californian land claims were to be subjected to review by the United States Government.

For the present all augured well. The Sepúlveda brothers had comfortable homes which they were constantly enlarging to accommodate their growing families, and their cattle business was prospering. When, on a January morning in 1848, gold was discovered at Coloma, they were swept into California's first fabulous period of prosperity—the halcyon days of the dons.

6

The Days of the Dons

CHRISTMAS, 1852, was the loveliest holiday Cesaria Sepúlveda had ever experienced.

The entire Sepúlveda family was invited to spend Navidad at the townhouse of their cousin José Andrés. For weeks she and Felipa had been supervising the Indian servants in sewing clothes for the occasion. Now there were great piles of beautiful garments made of the finest satin, velvet and brocade, all luxuriously ornamented with delicate lace or rich embroidery.

A week before Christmas day oxen were yoked to carretas, and the families of Juan and José Loreto started for Los Angeles. There were 13 children in all, a dozen servants, and the lovely Doñas Cesaria and Felipa.

Plenty of time had to be allowed for the trip, as it was the custom to visit at each ranch house along the way. First they stopped at the Ávila house, on the Rancho La Tajauta, next at the Lugo hacienda on Rancho San Antonio. Warm hospitality welcomed them at both homes, with lavish meals and much singing and dancing. Finally they arrived in the city on Christmas Eve.

The town had been swept clean of the rubbish that usually cluttered its narrow streets, and work was in progress on setting up the vendors' booths that were part of the celebration. The coming of the Americans had done little to change the old ways of the Angelenos. The Gold Rush had brought an influx of desperados and other riffraff, but it had also resulted in undreamed of prosperity. Never had there been a more resplendent Christmas!

Cesaria and Felipa stepped out of their carretas in front of the massive walled Sepúlveda residence, located near Eternity and Virgin Streets, away from the pandemonium of the Plaza. The house was a veritable beehive of activity. Servants were scurrying in all directions, a huge piñata was being hung in the patio, and in the grand sala Doña Sepúlveda was ensconced behind a magnificent silver tea service, pouring the afternoon *cha*.

Diego Sepúlveda, with his wife, Francisca Elizalde, and their three-month-old son, Aurelio, were already there. Laughter and talk resounded through the rooms, the younger children dashing in and out of doors, wild with excitement. Before long everyone decided to retire to prepare for the night's festivities.

That evening the Sepúlvedas joined the throng around the Plaza to watch Los Pastores, the traditional miracle play, enacted by the city's best amateur actors and musicians. The cool night air was filled with the pungent odor of tamales, enchiladas and tortillas being sold along with fruit and candy, from the many gaily decorated booths. The cries of the vendors mingled with music of guitars and violins and the voices of singers. Over all was the dominant clang of church bells. Not until the wee hours did the joyous fiesta come to a climax with fireworks and dancing in the Plaza common.

But at four o'clock in the morning everyone was assembled in the church for Christmas Mass. They were a dazzling array—the men in elegant velvet suits trimmed with gold fringe and metal buttons, the ladies in dresses so lavishly ornamented they could easily have stood alone. Outside were a large number of handsome horses, tied to the rail surrounding the Plaza, pawing and neighing impatiently as they waited for their masters. The first rays of the rising sun glinted on their splendid silver adornments when the long impressive service was over.

Fifteen-year-old Petra Pilar came out of the church wide-eyed at the dashing group of gay caballeros parading past. She didn't notice the darkly handsome young man who stood a few feet away, watching her with open admiration, until her father greeted him.

"Buenas días, Señor Lanfranco!" said José Loreto Sepúlveda, with a gracious bow. "Feliz Navidad!"

The courtly Italian merchant returned the courtesy and then murmured a charming compliment for Petra Pilar. Her lovely face suffused with blushes, she demurely lowered her eyes. Just then Don Antonio Lugo rode up on his beautiful black horse, mounted with resplendent silver saddle. The venerable old gentleman doffed his wide-brimmed hat and bowed deeply.

"Ah, mios amigos, such a beautiful day! All the world rejoices. Will I have the pleasure of seeing you at El Palacio?"

"But, of course!" replied José Loreto.

"Who would miss the reception at the home of Don Abel Stearns?" added Juan Lanfranco.

Soon everyone of any importance was assembled at the Stearns residence. Greeting their guests were Abel Stearns, a tall, dignified man of 54, with slightly greying hair and a vivid scar slashed across one cheek, and his beautiful, young wife, her huge violet eyes sparkling with the excitement of the affair.

Distributed through the elegantly appointed rooms were small groups, laughing, chatting and partaking of coffee, chocolate and delicious little sweetcakes. Daylight came in only dimly through the tall narrow windows, hung with lace curtains and heavy velvet drapes, but the house was brilliantly illuminated with a multitude of candles set in crystal chandeliers. Music from the large square piano, that had been brought around the Horn, provided a pleasant undercurrent of sound to the many happy voices.

Circulating from one group to another was an eager young American, the 22-year-old Phineas Banning, who had arrived in San Pedro only the year before. There were many matters he was anxious to discuss. In the short time he had been in California his aggressive drive had already made him an entrepreneur.

Although his main base of operation was San Pedro where he and his partner, Alexander, operated a lighterage and stagecoach service, his firm had expanded to the point where he had 500 mules, 40 horses, and freight wagons carrying goods as far as San Bernardino. Now, he wanted to line up support to solve some of the pressing problems that were preventing his business from prospering even more.

There were several barriers to the increase of trade at San Pedro. Probably the worst problem was that it was a not a port of entry. As a result, all foreign goods had to go to San Francisco. This, combined with the poor harbor that made lighterage necessary, caused exorbitantly high freight rates.

As soon as California was admitted to the Union in 1850, a Memorial had been sent to Senator Benton, requesting that San Pedro be made a port of entry. Banning had persuaded many influential citizens, including Abel Stearns, to write personal letters to the Senator urging him to follow up the Memorial. Still nothing had happened.

Another problem that worried Banning was California's isolation. There was no regular mail service. Letters arrived irregularly by boat, and mail sacks were simply dumped on the beach at San Pedro. Banning had been taking personal responsibility for getting them into Los Angeles at his own expense.

Relations between Phineas Banning and the Sepúlvedas had always been most amicable. Although the Sepúlvedas also had a stagecoach line, they ran it primarily as a matter of accommodation, as their main interest was in the cattle business. When August Timms bought the Sepúlveda Landing, earlier in the year, Banning was concerned. Timms was much more difficult to get along with than were the easygoing Juan and José Loreto. Now, Diego Sepúlveda had appeared on the San Pedro scene, and Banning wasn't sure what to expect.

It was rumored that Diego was one of the shrewdest men in California and could drive a hard bargain. The year before, he had sold his interest in the Rancho San Bernardino for a tidy sum and transferred operations to San Pedro. Juan and José Loreto had given him permission to graze his cattle on los Palos Verdes, but there was talk that he planned to raise sheep as well, and everyone knew that this was ruinous to pasture land.

Banning eyed Diego across the crowded sala. He was standing beside his wife, cooly aloof from the gathering. Banning made his way towards him.

"We haven't seen much of you yet at San Pedro, Señor," he said. "Is it true that you plan to reside there?"

"Indeed I do, Señor Banning!" he replied heartily. "I will soon have the first two-story adobe in that part of the country, the finest for miles around. There will be nothing to equal it."

"And you, Señora," Banning asked, "you will like living by the sea?"

Doña Sepúlveda tossing the long black curls which incongruously framed her sternly forbidding face.

"It will do," she said shortly.

Turning his attention back to Diego, Banning tried another gambit.

"Do you think we will have our customhouse at San Pedro?"

Diego's penetrating eyes swept over Banning.

"It's only a question of time," he stated flatly.

"Then we should look to developing the Inner Harbor," Banning said. "We have to make it possible for large ships to enter easily and tie up safely."

Diego raised his sweeping black brows and snorted.

"That's a ridiculous idea! The expense of dredging a channel would be prohibitive. Where's the money to come from?"

His sharp eyes narrowed. "If you want to look to the future, you had better build your own wharf at San Pedro. That's where the business is and always will be."

Banning shrugged. "I'll have to talk to Juan and José about selling me some land, I guess."

Diego gave him a canny smile. "I'm sure they would be willing." Then he added softly, "You should stay with the lighterage business. There's too much competition in running stagecoaches."

Through the window Banning saw the beautiful Lugo coach pulling up before the house. He smiled but said nothing. Soon he would have a surprise for Diego, and August Timms as well. There would be real competition!

Now, the gala function at El Palacio was ending. Juan and José Loreto were collecting their families to return to the Sepúlveda residence for the rest of the day's festivities. It was a long time before they located Petra Pilar. She and Juan Lanfranco were sitting quietly in the long covered corridor outside, deep in conversation.

Even greater prosperity came to the Sepúlvedas with the coming of the New Year. Prices soared as the demand for beef cattle continued to increase. Before the Gold Rush, hides sold for about two dollars each and tallow for six to eight cents a pound. Now one steer brought from fifty to seventy dollars.

Juan and José prepared for the long cattle drive north to San Francisco. They did not need to make the trip themselves, as a major-domo and Indian vaqueros handled the herds. Still there was always the danger of a stampede or a raid by thieves and it seemed wise to go along and protect their investment. Besides it was a lovely route at this time of the year, across the Tehachapi Mountains and along the San Joaquin Valley to San Jose and the Bay area.

They were part of a large and distinguished company of Southern California rancheros, all of whom made it a point to be back by the middle of February to attend Abel Stearns' grand ball celebrating Washington's birthday. This was an occasion for great excitement in the Sepúlveda household, as it was Petra Pilar's first ball.

On the evening of the event, she was dressed and breathless with anticipation long before it was time to go the short distance from the Ávila house to El Palacio. As she entered the glittering, 100-foot ballroom, accompanied by Doña Felipa and Cesaria, she made an entrancing picture: richly embroidered white satin skirt standing out around her, shining black hair in curls at her temples, and a single crimson rose tucked behind one tiny ear.

Immediately Juan Lanfranco approached, his eyes aglow with admiration. Bowing low, he requested Doña Sepúlveda's permission to dance with her daughter. Then he took her small hand in his and the couple was swept away to the gay music of the fandango.

All evening Lanfranco never took his eyes off the happy animated features of Petra Pilar. He listened with rapt attention to every word she said and gazed into the luminous depths of her eyes with the look of a drowning man. Cesaria, watching from the side of the room where she sat with the other Doñas, smiled knowingly and sighed a bit. It would not be long before she would lose her first-born daughter.

Towards midnight when the dancing was at its height, suddenly there was a tremendous commotion at the door leading to the street. Before the horrified eyes of the assembled company, the door was battered down and the nose of a cannon thrust into the room. Then several masked bandits came crashing in, brandishing knives and pistols.

Instantly the guest nearest the door whipped out his revolver and shot one of the intruders. The firing became general and a wild cacophony of screams and shouts filled the house. Finally the raiders were beaten back into the street. So commonplace was this occurrence in the Los Angeles of the 1850s, that within a few minutes the festivities were resumed.

Soon after the Gold Rush began Los Angeles became the toughest and most lawless city west of Santa Fe. Gamblers, outlaws and prostitutes flowed into the city, following the scent of big money, lavishly spent. On Calle de los Negros, a few feet from the Plaza, gamblers guarded tables piled with gold ready to beat and kick into the alley any patron who protested being stripped of his wealth.

Horse stealing, highway robbery and murder were everyday events. One newspaper editor wrote: "On Tuesday of last week we had four weddings, two funerals, one street fight with knives, a lynch court, two men flogged, a fist fight and a man tossed in a blanket."

Responsible citizens finally decided to take action. One July day in 1853, a group of leading townsmen met in the El Dorado Saloon on

Main Street and organized the Los Angeles Rangers. This was a semi-vigilante, semi-social organization, which did much to stem the tide of crime and violence in the city. Nevertheless, despite their efforts, Los Angeles kept its wicked reputation for almost two decades.

This did little to disturb the splendid life of the rancheros or the march of Yankee enterprise. Traffic between Los Angeles and San Pedro was brisk. More and more ships were putting into the harbor, and the stagecoach business was on the increase.

Frequently, races were held between the stages of Banning, Timms and the Sepúlvedas. Because of the rickety construction of the coaches, the rough road and the wildness of the horses, the ride was always full of thrills. But, when a race was on, it was death-defying, the passengers hanging on for dear life at the same time that they were cheerfully placing their bets.

Normally the ride between San Pedro and the Bella Union Hotel, on Main Street, in Los Angeles, took a couple of hours. A race could cut the time substantially. The fastest trip on record was made in one hour and eighteen minutes, including three changes of horses.

For a long time, Phineas Banning had had an idea that would give his firm an advantage over its competitors. Used to the beautiful Concord coaches of the East, four-wheeled, sturdy, and incredibly comfortable, he wanted to import some. Longingly he looked at the only two in Southern California; one belonging to Abel Stearns, the other to the wealthy Lugo family. The coaches cost over 1000 dollars apiece and required expensive horses. But Banning thought it worth the gamble. He placed an order for four.

Meanwhile word came from Washington that San Pedro would soon have a customhouse. Banning had been negotiating with the Sepúlvedas for a tract of land on the beach near Timms' Landing. Promptly he consummated the deal and built his own wharf. When the news came that Congress had passed the bill designating San Pedro a Port of Entry, he was fully prepared.

One night that summer crates were brought ashore secretly, and the handsome coaches assembled in the Banning-Alexander warehouse. Resplendently dressed for the occasion, Banning himself drove the first coachload of passengers into Los Angeles. When he arrived at the Bella Union Hotel, word spread through the city like wildfire. People were amazed and delighted. Soon the vehicles were running on a regular schedule.

Everyone wanted a ride on the new coaches. They carried nine passengers inside, and ten to twelve outside. Space was provided for lugggage under the driver's seat and at the rear of the coach.

Once in San Pedro, it was natural to stop at the offices of Banning's firm. As a result his shipping and commission business increased daily. Gratified at his success the great showman decided on a fabulous publicity stunt. The funloving Californians thrived on fiestas. Why not a really gala celebration for the Fourth of July?

Large quantities of food, wine and fireworks were ordered from San Francisco and, days before the Fourth, the clipper ship *Laura Bevan* put into San Pedro laden with supplies for the gigantic party. Invitations were passed by word of mouth and published in the Los Angeles *Star*. Everyone was invited, from Santa Barbara to San Diego, and as far east as San Bernardino.

On the morning of July 3rd Banning's coaches were lined up at the Plaza to take people, free of charge, to San Pedro. Over and over they returned to transport more passengers. In addition, every possible conveyance was pressed into service. Some families came in their gaily decorated carretas and there were long lines of splendidly mounted caballeros.

By nightfall two thousand guests were assembled in San Pedro. There were neither houses nor beds for them. But no one was concerned. From the moment of their arrival, everyone was involved in a continuous round of merry-making. An enormous dining table was kept going all night, musicians and dancers took turns, and those who were not eating or dancing were busy exchanging toasts, making speeches or singing patriotic songs.

Naturally, the households of Juan and José Loreto Sepúlveda were in a turmoil dispensing hospitality to close friends and relatives. Happy greetings rang out as they saw some people for the first time in years. Petra Pilar glowed with pride and happiness as her fiance, Juan Lanfranco, drove up in his fashionable conveyance, the pioneer sulky he had bought in San Francisco.

The next morning there was a grand parade at the harbor. Brilliant sunlight beat down on the mudflats, a sapphire sea, and the lovely *Laura Bevan* lying at anchor, as over a thousand patriots marched around the newly erected flag pole from which floated the Stars and Stripes. They then formed a huge hollow square, and each participant was provided with a bottle of champagne, the cork already pulled, and a glass.

Now Banning's partner, George Alexander, stepped forward and requested the attention of the gathering. He spoke slowly and forcefully, an interpreter translating his words into Spanish.

"Gentlemen, I will give a toast which when drunk will be followed by three cheers. Gentlemen, here is to the President of the United States."

Every man drank, and three tremendous cheers sounded and resounded, echoing back from the burnt-brown-sienna hills of los Palos Verdes. Other toasts followed to Banning and the Alexanders, and to the future of San Pedro.

Later in the day, Juan Sepúlveda announced that a large boat stood ready to take those who wished to go to Dead Man's Island for a special ceremony. On board was the famous little bronze cannon, "the old woman's gun," which had played such an important part in the American invasion a scant seven years before. During the interval it had remained buried near Juan's house.

When the boat reached the island, the venerable piece of artillery was carried with great difficulty up the steep slopes to the highest point on the barren rock. There it was fired, letting loose a great roar. Then in ringing tones Juan Sepúlveda addressed the assembled throng.

He recounted the story of the battle in which the seven sailors, before whose wooden headboards they stood, had been killed and explained that the salvo just fired had a triple purpose. It should serve as a salute to these brave mariners who had lost their lives in the service of their country, it should dissipate the last vestiges of ill feeling towards the Americans, and it should express the gratitude of all Californians to the great founders of modern liberty.

Finally, with characteristic warmhearted exuberance, he tossed back his head and cried:

"Viva Los Estados Unidos! Viva México! Somos Amigos!"

The crowd roared its approval. Then after much libation, cheering and congratulating each other, the assemblage embarked for the mainland. There festivities continued for the rest of that day, all night and most of the fifth. Gradually, sleepy and worn out, people started back to Los Angeles. This had been an affair long to be remembered.

A day or two after the Fourth of July celebration, there was again much cause for excitement at los Palos Verdes. First Juan Lanfranco arrived at the home of Petra Pilar, his elegant suit torn and bedraggled, a sheepish look on his handsome face. On his way home from the festivities, he had been thrown from his carriage, landing on the roadside.

Next the Sepúlvedas' major-domo rode up to the house, his whole troop of vaqueros at his heels, seemingly scared out of their wits.

"The devil himself has got among the manadas," gasped the major-domo.

"A phantom! A phantom!" yelled the vaqueros.

"En el nombre de Dios, take hold of yourself man and tell me what is the matter?" said José Loreto sternly.

The major-domo shook his head. "I do not know, señor. Something has gotten among the herds, a kind of what-is-it. The horses are running wild and the cattle as well, those of Domínguez, Lugo and Ávila, not just our own."

"But why hasn't something been done?" demanded Sepúlveda.

"We have tried, señor," replied the major-domo shamefacedly. "But we can do nothing. They are terrified and so are the vaqueros."

With a gesture of impatience, Sepúlveda ordered his horse saddled and brought. Just then one of Lugo's men galloped up to the door. He was grinning broadly.

"Do not disturb yourself, señor. It is all over. We have found the phantom.

He glanced at Juan Lanfranco and laughed uproariously. "And your sulky as well."

When Juan had been thrown from his carriage, the gay old mustang hitched to the sulky, feeling himself free, had taken to his old game of chasing the herds. Frightened at the strange apparition, they had gone wild and the mustang, astonished at such unfriendliness, had chased the harder. In no time the great stampede was well under way.

For a long time the "phantom tarantula" was the byword and joke of the day!

Life at los Palos Verdes remained wrapped in a golden bubble of pastoral peace and plenty. San Pedro, with neither streets not buildings, was a sleepy barren place, except for the bustling activity at the harbor. Each day the port acquired more status as the shipping center of the southwest. Because of this Diego Sepúlveda hastened to secure his holdings there.

He was in a good position to do so. The year before, Juan and José had filed a declaration of trust stating that, although the title to los Palos Verdes was in their names, they recognized both Diego and the heirs of Teresa as having a right equal to their own to the property.

The fact that Diego had deeded his interest in los Palos Verdes to Santiago Johnson in exchange for the San Bernardino property bothered him not at all. Moving rapidly, he established himself at the San Pedro end of the Peninsula. He put up a commission office on the bluff and a warehouse on the beach below. Then he proceeded to build his hacienda, a magnificent adobe, at what is today the corner of Channel and Gaffey Streets.

Generous, easygoing Juan and José Sepúlveda were not concerned. In fact, for José and Cesaria, everything was dwarfed by furious preparation for the wedding of their daughter, Petra Pilar. The Sepúlveda haciendas were readied to receive guests from as far away as a 100 miles for the weeklong festivities. Elaborate gowns were handsewn and enormous quantities of food prepared. Last, but not least, was the making of the cascarones.

This was a delicate operation. Tiny holes were made in eggs and their contents blown out. Then with painstaking care, the shells were filled with finely-cut pieces of gilt paper and immersed in perfume. The last step was to seal the perforations with wax and decorate the eggs in gay colors. During the wedding fandango, gallant gentlemen and dazzling señoritas would break the cascarones over each others' heads as tokens of admiration and flirtation.

On the eve of the wedding, José Loreto Sepúlveda's sprawling adobe sparkled from days of sweeping, polishing and adorning. Two large wings extended back from the three elegant front rooms, comprising bedrooms, kitchen facilities and servants' quarters. A high wall across the rear formed an interior courtyard or patio, with wide corredors on the three sides of the house. It was an ideal setting for the wedding fiesta, easily accommodating well over a hundred guests.

The only calm person in the household was Petra Pilar. She was too happy to be concerned about the bustling activitiy. That morning she had received her bridal gifts from Juan Lanfranco. As was the custom, he had sent three complete changes of costume. And as an additional token of his devotion, they were packed in roses, the flower that signified, "thou art the queen of thy sex."

The lovingly selected garments were from among the choicest imported treasures available in the city. This fine raiment was to be for the celebrations at los Palos Verdes. According to tradition, Petra Pilar would wear simple apparel for the ceremony in the Plaza Church.

In the late afternoon she journeyed to Los Angeles, accompanied by her immediate family, and very early the next morning the nuptial Mass took place. As the couple emerged from the church, they were exuberantly greeted by music and a gay group of friends, who bore them triumphantly to the Sepúlveda townhouse, where a sumptuous breakfast was served.

Then the bride and groom were escorted to los Palos Verdes in a jubilant parade with music, elaborately decorated carretas and splendidly mounted caballeros making up the line of march. There guests sat down to a beautifully appointed table loaded with delicacies. Soon Petra Pilar joined them, wearing the first of her wedding costumes, a gown of white brocaded silk, with shawl embroidered in sprays of pink roses.

After dinner part of the company retired to rest, while the younger members of the crowd danced in the patio. All afternoon, and well into the evening, people continued to arrive for the celebration. A long table was set up in the courtyard for prominent guests; the others feasted beneath the trees, cooking their own steaks.

By midnight the fandango was in full swing. Sparkling señoritas, richly dressed rancheros, fashionable gamblers, store clerks, county officials and well-to-do merchants all intermingled to the music of harp, guitar and violins. Many a gay cavalier and his lovely lady were drenched with perfume and covered with the glittering contents of a cascarone. Not until dawn did the brilliant show end.

And this was only the beginning of the festivities. For days the fiesta continued with dancing every night and horseracing and bullfighting the daytime amusements. Juan Lanfranco was happy to see the week of revelry finally draw to a close. It had been difficult for him to wait patiently as he gazed upon the lovely tender face of his beloved. He was anxious to take his bride to her new home in the city.

After the wedding life at los Palos Verdes settled into its normal activites, ranching, trading, shipping and staging. Ships en route from San Diego to San Francisco made San Pedro a port-of-call. A regular run between San Pedro and San Francisco was established, with the *Laura Bevan* and the *Sea Serpent* carrying both freight and passengers. And Abel Stearns put his clipper ship, the *Arcadia*, into service to Boston. Meanwhile the stagecoach business became highly competitive.

Although Banning and Alexander led the field, Timms, Tomlinson and Diego Sepúlveda were hard on their heels. Each tried to outdo the other in rates, routes and running time. Neck and neck races between rivals provided fast and exciting rides, and the fares continued to drop— from ten dollars to five, and finally to fifty cents.

Everyone was talking about Diego Sepúlveda's new house. It was a large two-story adobe, with upper veranda. Two beautiful pepper trees planted in front were to become a landmark in the area. Furnishings were the finest that could be imported from the East and the Orient.

Handsome bureaus, inlaid tables, brocade sofas, velvet drapes, Oriental rugs, gilt-framed tapestries, and a rosewood piano were part of the luxurious appointments.

Far from resenting their brother's affluence, Juan and José equated his interests with their own. When in 1851 the United States Land Commission was established to review the validity of all Spanish or Mexican land grants, they had taken prompt action to defend the Sepúlvedas' claim. Well within the time limits provided, they had filed for los Palos Verdes.

Receiving notice of confirmation of their claim, on December 10, 1853, they had reason to think all was well. But built into the Land Act was the provision for appeal by the government to the courts. Immediately the Sepúlvedas were notified that their case had been appealed to the District Court. That the reasons were flimsy, and even inaccurate, only added to the brothers' frustration.

The appeal procedure dragged on for three years. Juan and José bore the brunt of the tremendous expense and inconvenience involved. Diego Sepúlveda was having troubles of his own making.

In November of 1853 the heirs of Santiago Johnson brought suit for the one-fifth interest in the Rancho de los Palos Verdes which Diego had deeded in exchange for his San Bernardino property. Judgment was rendered in favor of the Johnsons, and Diego was ordered to relinquish the land and pay over 500 dollars in costs and damages. Thus the first piece of los Palos Verdes was lost to the Sepúlvedas. Twenty years later, Jotham Bixby was to pick up this land at a public auction.

By the summer of 1855, new problems had been added to the burdens of the Sepúlvedas. The bottom had started to fall out of the cattle market. Large numbers of both cattle and sheep were being driven into California from Missouri, Texas and Mexico. The price of beef began a downward spiral as spectacular as had been its rise following the Gold Rush.

Feeling the financial strain of costly court proceedings and unable to convert their herds into ready cash, Juan and Felipa Sepúlveda took the first step in the direction that was to lead to their loss of los Palos Verdes. On May 11, 1855, they mortgaged their one-fifth interest in the Rancho to secure payment of a note for $2,962.86. Interest on the note was six percent per month!

The golden bubble was about to burst.

7

End of an Era

FOUR YEARS BEFORE that fateful summer in 1855, when the Sepúlvedas'
hold on los Palos Verdes began to slip, the first representatives of the
family who would someday own their land left Maine for California.

It was the clarion call of gold that brought Llewellyn Bixby and
his cousin, Thomas Flint, across the Isthmus and up the coast to San Francisco. But as the battered, old *S.S. Northerner* sailed past the Palos Verdes
Peninsula, Llewellyn looked with longing on the rich grazing meadows
and rolling hills and determined to possess a portion of this land. Some
years of hard work and shrewd trading, abetted by fortuitous turns of
fortune's wheel, were to pass before his dream was realized.

Now his destination was the Volcano diggings in the western foothills
of the Sierra. Arriving there, early in July, 1851, he was somewhat shocked
by the rough brawling mining camp, so unlike the New England decorum
to which he was accustomed. One week in the mines was quite enough
for his conservative personality. Preferring the sureness of stated wages
to the uncertain promise of gold, he took a job in the local butcher shop
at 150 dollars a month and "keep." The latter held particular appeal
for his thrifty disposition, because of the high cost of living.

The following year, Llewellyn was joined by his brothers, Marcellus
and Jotham. Within a matter of months, the three Bixbys and Flint

owned the butcher business and were involved in several other mercantile enterprises in the tiny town. They were accumulating gold fast. Towards the end of 1852, they had enough to take the next big step toward fame and fortune.

On Christmas Day they left for home, with the objective of bringing a herd of sheep across the continent to California. Foregoing the comfort of first-class passage from San Francisco to New York, they embarked steerage, again on the old tub, the *S.S. Northerner.* To save the expense of shipping their hoard of gold, they carried it with them in buckskin jackets especially made for that purpose. Finding the weight of the heavy gold slugs too much for constant carrying, they appropriated a vacant stateroom, put the treasure between two mattresses and took turns guarding it night and day.

Down to Panama, across the Isthmus and up the Atlantic seaboard, they wended their careful way. Twenty-seven days out of San Francisco, they arrived in New York and proceeded immediately to Philadelphia, where their gold was assayed and deposited. A little more than a month later, they were once again on the road.

It was a long difficult journey by rail, horseback, emigrant wagon and on foot. Frequently they covered only a few miles a day. Along the way they bought sheep, finding a few at one place, a few at another, struggling to amalgamate the little groups into one homogenous band. At Warsaw, Illinois, while still buying stock, they thriftily sheared their sheep and sold 6,410 pounds of wool for $1,570.45. Finally they had gathered a flock numbering well over 2000.

By early September they were in Salt Lake City, where they took advantage of the Mormons' warm hospitality to rest and recuperate for three weeks. The hardest part of the trip was still ahead of them: stony trails, dust, days without food or water for the animals, a thorny world of sagebrush and cactus. It was with enormous thanksgiving that they reached the comparative comfort of the Mojave River late in December, camping on dry bur clover and anticipating a mess of quail for Christmas dinner.

On New Year's Day, ten months after the start of their journey, they were safely in San Bernardino, and a few days later they arrived at the Rancho San Pasqual, the site of present-day Pasadena, which they rented to pasture their herds for the winter. Spring saw them on the move again northward past Santa Barbara and across the mountains to Paso Robles, San Luis Obispo and San Jose. There they rented the Rancho Santa Teresa for fourteen months.

In 1855, they moved to Monterey County and bought the 54,000-acre Rancho San Justo near San Juan Bautista. For forty years, this ranch was to be the headquarters for Flint, Bixby and Company, the firm organized by the family while en route across the United States. The sheep business had proved profitable beyond the Bixbys' fondest dreams. Now they were firmly established in California. But it would be another ten years before their empire spread to the southern part of the state.

These were ten tragic years for all Southern California rancheros. Their troubles started with the Land Act of 1851. Both before and after the American conquest, official and unofficial spokesmen for the United States had assured Californians that the government would safeguard existing land titles and respect all rights of private property. But the law which Congress passed challenged the validity of every title in California!

The reasons for the debacle are understandable in retrospect. Complete bedlam resulted from the enormous emigration of gold seekers. There was no time properly to replace simple Spanish-Mexican customs with Anglo-American laws. Having discovered that prospecting was hard and often unr⸗ ⸗arding, disappointed emigrants demanded fertile farm lands. A harried Congress, thousands of miles away, with no means for obtaining accurate, up-to-date information, acted with no comprehension of the bewildering California scene.

By placing the burden of proof upon the Spanish-Mexican grantees, the law that they framed further inflamed the minds of landhungry settlers, already loath to respect the property rights of a people for whom they had a traditional contempt. Squatters did not hesitate to occupy any land under litigation. Meanwhile the rancheros struggled in a mass of sticky legal maneuvering which they didn't understand, and which sucked up any capital they had or could obtain.

Abel Stearns, one of the wealthiest and most powerful men in California, wrote in despair to John C. Frémont: "The long lists of Sheriffs' and mortgage sales in our newspapers, the depopulation of flourishing stock Ranchos, and the pauperism of Rancheros, but a short time since wealthy, all attest to the disastrous consequences of too much litigation."

As if the endless trials ensuing from the Land Act were not enough to bankrupt the rancheros, they had other problems. The seven glory years of easy money and lavish spending which they had experienced resulted in an extravagance and financial ineptitude bordering on irresponsibility. Accustomed to a situation in which they could obtain money on the basis of a smile, a handshake, and their word of honor, they signed inequitable short-term mortgages, at impossible interest rates, without the faintest idea of what they were doing.

They might still have been able to weather through the storm, but the very framework of their existence collapsed with the prolonged and desperate depression in the cattle industry. The importation of stock from other states as well as the institution of cattle farms for the breeding of livestock soon glutted the market. The new bonanza was in sheep, and later in agriculture. The majority of the rancheros couldn't make the transition.

The Sepúlvedas' tribulations were multiplied by treacherous rivalry and bickering within their own family.

A couple of months after Juan and Felipa Sepúlveda were forced to mortgage their interest in los Palos Verdes, their nephew, Pablo Pryor, sued ''to recover'' his two-fifths interest in the Rancho. There was no need for him to do this, as there was no question about his claim. Fifteen years before, Ygnacio Sepúlveda had surrendered his one-fifth interest to Pablo's father. The other fifth had been deeded to his mother by Juan and José's magnanimous Declaration of Trust.

The 17-year-old boy, orphaned since the death of Nathaniel Pryor in 1850, had become something of a misanthrope. Without a home of his own, he had come to feel alone and neglected. Of course a judgment was rendered in his favor. But, untrained and inept, he had no way to hold on to the land. Within the next ten years, he sold half of it to Phineas Banning and the rest to the I.J. Tomlinson Company. For each parcel he received $3000.

Phineas Banning's fortunes had continued to increase. To him it seemed a propitious time to bring his dream of extending San Pedro Harbor to fruition. For years he had been exploring the Inner Slough, making notes and crude sketches. Though many people ridiculed his ideas he was sure that, if a channel were dredged to the Inner Harbor back of Rattlesnake Island, the tides would keep it free of sand. Big ships could then be tied up to wharves built on the shore. This would do away with the expense of lighterage, and goods could be landed quickly and easily.

In November of 1854 the following notice appeared in a Southern California newspaper:

> We understand that several capitalists of this place have effected a purchase of twenty-four hundred acres on the creek six miles this side of San Pedro, with the intention of laying out a new city. With some expense the creek can be made as good a harbor as is on the Pacific Coast; and in case the Pacific Railroad makes its terminus in this valley,

it will be directed to this point and build up a city of considerable importance and enrich the gentlemen who have embarked on this new enterprise.

For a little more than a dollar an acre, Phineas Banning, J.G. Downey,
Don Benito Wilson and William Sanford had purchased from Manuel
Domínguez, 2400 acres of the Rancho San Pedro, bordering the bay
immediately back of Rattlesnake Island. The first step toward the building
of the multimillion dollar Los Angeles Harbor had been taken.

For Juan and José Sepúlveda, the year 1856 brought no relief from
financial distress. In the spring, Juan and Felipa were so pressed that
they deeded their fifth of los Palos Verdes to a man by the name of
Lamalfa for $5000. Lamalfa in turn took out a couple of short-term mort-
gages on the land at an interest rate of 4 per cent per month. A year
later the mortgages were foreclosed, and in the Sheriff's sale that ensued,
Diego Sepúlveda picked up the property for about $3000!

Meanwhile the legal battle for title to the land continued. On
December 10, 1856, the District Court confirmed the Sepúlvedas' claim
to the Rancho de los Palos Verdes. But immediately the case was appealed
to the Supreme Court. Because the land grant was bestowed in the names
of Juan and José, it was their responsibility to carry on the endless,
debilitating litigation.

Christmas of 1857 was very different for Cesaria Sepúlveda from
the joyous Navidads of former years. It was hard to enter into the
festivities. There was so much hard feeling in the family, and her heart
ached for Juan and Felipa. They still lived in their comfortable home,
but stripped of their land they had lost all status.

José spent hours with Juan, trying to figure out how to stem the
tide of adversity which threatened to destroy their livelihood. To add
to their worries, the winter of 1857-58 brought very little rain, and their
cattle were showing the effects of the resulting food and water shortage.
Attempts to sell them brought only bitter disappointment.

Early in 1858, José persuaded Diego to enter into a plan designed,
at least partially, to restore Juan's battered pride. Together they deeded
a small portion of the Rancho de los Palos Verdes back to him. It was
the property on which stood his house.

The sons of Juan and José, some in their early teens, had little to
do in the rapidly dwindling activities of the Rancho. In the winter months
they spent hours watching the fascinating whaling operations at Portuguese Bend, Rocky Point and Malaga Cove. Often they wished they
could join in the thrilling adventures enacted before their eyes.

Enterprising New Englanders had instituted the whaling industry early in the 1800s. The dangerous but lucrative practice of shore whaling developed in 1851, under the leadership of Captain C.M. Scammon. Soon there was a string of eleven whaling stations along the California coast, from Half Moon Bay to Point Abanda in Baja California. One of these was at Portuguese Bend.

It came to be called this because most of the whalers were Portuguese. A hardy happy-go-lucky lot, they sailed into San Pedro every winter and, with their boats and gear, headed for the Bend. Their prey was the gray whale, a species that migrated from the Bering Sea and Arctic Ocean to breeding grounds in warm southern waters between the months of November and May.

On a warm sunny morning in March, nineteen-year-old Julián yielded to the coaxing of his cousins, Juan Bautista and Francisco, and asked José Sepúlveda's permission to take the boys down to Portuguese Bend. As they rode over the terraced slopes of the Palos Verdes Hills, they could see the whaling boats lying along the kelp below; their colored sails gaily decorated with strange and wondrous emblems designating the vessels to which they belonged.

Approaching the cove, the stench of oil and blubber hit their nostrils, but to them it was the scent of excitement. A crude shack stood at the base of the cliff. In it were the washroom, the dryingroom, a small storeroom and the cooper's shop. Outside were two enormous copper kettles set in a rude furnace, formed of rocks and clay, in which the whale fat was being tried out. Next to these, to receive the blubber, were huge vats made of planks. Thick black clouds of smoke rose from the scrap-fire under the steaming kettles.

Several men were flensing the catch of the night before, a forty-five-foot female, almost thirty feet in circumference. A couple of them shoved and hauled on a sort of capstan, which served to roll the carcass, while others stripped off the fat. The mutilated whale was a mass of blood and blubber, and around it hovering gulls drowned out the sound of the surf with their piercing screams.

Suddenly the shouts of the lookout man, stationed on the bluff above, cut through the noise. Everyone stopped work to watch. He had sighted a whale!

Dipping his flag, he signaled the boats the direction of their quarry. Slowly the boats turned, signaling back by dipping the peaks of their sails. Fifteen-year-old Francisco was so excited he could hardly contain himself. If only he could be out there on one of those boats!

Holding his breath, he saw one of them approach within striking distance of where the mammoth creature had just appeared. Then before his horrified gaze, the whale thrashed about and with his ponderous flukes upset the boat, splintering its keel. At the same moment, he saw a second whale surface close by!

The men on shore were already shoving off to the rescue. Before Julián could stop him, Francisco leaped on board. Oblivious to the danger involved, his only thought was to help catch one of the devilfish.

Shouting at the top of his voice, he managed to make himself heard, finally getting the attention of the distraught whalers. As they pulled their boat up between the huge animals and the rescue operation, fortunately, one of the whales sounded and disappeared. The other surfaced again.

Taking careful aim, the gunner fired. Struck, the whale started to run. Desperately, the men tried to hold onto the line and at the same time haul up to the animal in order to shoot a bomb-lance into a vital part. When the bomb was shot it failed to explode!

Now the whale sounded, hauling the bow of the boat under the water. Instantly the men let out the line, slowly slacking it. If the whale didn't surface again immediately, the line would have to be cut, or the boat would be pulled under. Frantically Francisco tried to help hang onto the line, feeling it burn as it tore through his fingers.

Then with a gasp of relief, he saw the whale "bring to" about twenty feet from the boat. But it rolled from side to side and thrashed the water with its enormous flukes. For the first time, Francisco was really frightened. To his amazement, the whalers seemed suddenly almost jovial.

Gradually the boat was drawn closer and closer to the whale. A second bomb-lance was shot. Then a third. The latter did the fatal work. Now, the prize had only to be towed to shore.

By the time this was accomplished, the rest of the whalers had embarked for San Pedro with the men who had been hurt in the accident. One had suffered a broken arm, another a head wound, and the third bruises and lacerations. Julián had ridden ahead to summon help. Juan Bautista was waiting for Francisco.

As the elder brother, he knew he should give him a stiff dressing-down for his escapade. But seeing his face aglow with excitement, and overcome with gratitude for his safety, Juan hadn't the heart to scold him. In these troubled days, there was little enough to satisfy a young boy's thirst for adventure. Quietly, the brothers mounted their horses and rode back to the ranchhouse, each occupied with his own thoughts.

On the 4th of March, 1858, the Supreme Court rendered its deci-

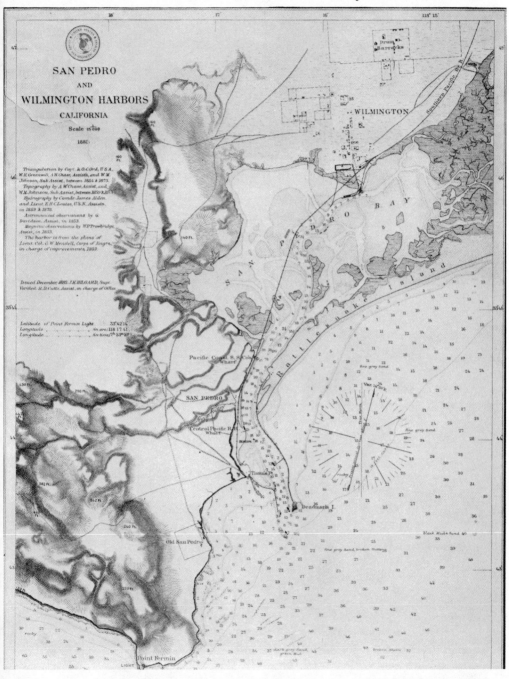

Map of San Pedro and Wilmington Harbors, 1883. U.S. Coast and Geodetic Survey.
(Reproduction by permission of the Huntington Library, San Marino, California)

Home of Florence Dodson Schoneman, granddaughter of Diego Sepúlveda, daughter of Rudecínda Sepúlveda Dodson. Circa 1900, San Pedro. *(Courtesy of the Seaver Center for Western History Research, Natural History Museum of Los Angeles County)*

El Palacio, the home of Abel Stearns, was the social center of the Pueblo of Los Angeles in the early 1850s. This photograph was taken about 1875, shortly before the adobe was torn down. *(Reproduction by permission of The Huntington Library, San Marino, California)*

San Pedro Harbor entrance about 1886; now freight and passenger trains could reach deep water. *(Courtesy of the Seaver Center for Western History Research Natural History Museum of Los Angeles County)*

San Pedro Harbor, about 1895. Early Custom House (with flag) in foreground. *(Courtesy of the Seaver Center for Western History Research, Natural History Museum of Los Angeles County)*

Harbor Celebration—the fight for a free harbor had been won, April 1899. *(Courtesy of the Seaver Center for Western History Research, Natural History Museum of Los Angeles County)*

San Pedro, about 1903. Front Street, now Harbor Boulevard.
Building at top of hill was the Carnegie Library. Telephone
poles and steaming engines attest to the economic growth of
the area. *(Courtesy of the Seaver Center for Western History
Research, Natural History Museum of Los Angeles County)*

San Pedro Harbor—no date.
(Courtesy of the Seaver Center for
Western History Research,
Natural History Museum of Los Angeles County)

Looking easterly up the Main Channel and showing the east San Pedro ferry landings, about 1903. Train on trestle in background holding rock for jetty. *(Courtesy of the Seaver Center for Western History Research, Natural History Museum of Los Angeles County)*

sion relative to the Sepúlveda claim to los Palos Verdes. Once again it was favorable, but nothing was settled. Twenty-two years of tangled litigation followed before the United States Government issued the formal patent to the land on June 23, 1880.

The delay was caused by an unprecedented number of legal actions: partition suits, foreclosure actions, suits to eject squatters, condemnation proceedings and divorces—78 lawsuits in all. A large portion of these were instituted by internecine quarreling among the Sepúlvedas themselves. But the root of the problem was buried far beneath the level of family feuding.

The cancerous growth which destroyed a whole way of life stemmed from a desperate need for money. By 1860 the standard price of breeding cows had fallen to ten dollars a head, and the market had dwindled to a fourth of what it was in former years. A series of natural disasters followed, which added to the rancheros' almost unbearable burdens.

Late in 1861 an unprecedented storm set in. For a month rain came down in tropical torrents. Dry creeks were turned into raging rivers. Helplessly the Sepúlvedas watched while the flood-waters mounted.

They were never able to ascertain the exact number of cattle they lost. But ironically, this was not the most serious consequence of the storm. The heavy rains transformed grazing land into lush meadows. During the ensuing year, their herds multiplied to record proportions, but the glutted market would not absorb them. Prices broke to even lower levels.

Then during the fall and winter of 1862, there was no rain. The huge herds had little food or water. Business in Los Angeles was practically paralyzed. To further complicate matters, a smallpox epidemic started in the fall and ravaged the whole of Southern California throughout the winter. Juan and José were desperate.

By spring their cattle were starving. Harsh scorching winds swept in from the desert, bringing millions of grasshoppers to further devastate the desolate land. Prayerfully, they waited for the long hot summer to pass and the blessing of the rainy season to come. But fall slipped into winter, and winter into spring and still there was no relief.

Day after day, they rode over the Rancho, looking with heavy hearts on their once robust livestock, now lying listlessly about on the parched earth, gasping for water. Finally, the inevitable decision was reached. They would have to slaughter the sickest for the trifling value of their hides and horns.

Even then, they were unprepared for the rapidity with which the cattle market was spiraling downward. A large hide brought only two dollars and a half, and the cost of skinning the animal reduced the net return to 25 cents!

One day in the middle of February, as Juan and José were supervising the dismal business of stripping and stretching hides to cure on the beach, suddenly they felt a few drops of rain. Forgetting the dignity of their fifty years, they tossed their hats into the air and danced with excitement, like boys in their teens. For two days, a generous rain fell, and great was the rejoicing throughout the country. But it was short-lived.

The brief storm was followed by dry, electrical north winds, heat and desiccating dust. Any slight beneficial effect of the rain was wiped out. Once again the Sepúlvedas looked upon an iron earth and a sky of brass.

Before long, all of the land between Los Angeles and the sea was covered with heaps of skeletons bleaching in the blazing sun. In April of 1864, a local newspaper stated: "The cattle of Los Angeles County are dying so fast for want of food that the large rancheros keep their men busily employed in obtaining hides. Thousands of carcasses strew the plains in all directions a short distance from the city, and the sight is harrowing in extreme."

Between 1862 and 1864, the number of cattle in the country decreased by 71 per cent. Tax assessments on range land fell from 25 to 10 cents an acre. Still five-sixths of the land was reported tax delinquent. Now many rancheros, including the Sepúlvedas, were offering cattle for as little as a dollar and a half a head, and there were no buyers.

The delinquent-tax lists contained most of the prominent landowners of Los Angeles County. Those who had for so long valiantly fought for their land were finally defeated by the great drought. From the plains and rolling hills disappeared the thousands of cattle which had once carried the familiar brands of the proudest families in California. Soon their owners' vast estates would pass forever into alien hands.

Meanwhile, the indomitable Phineas Banning continued to thrive. By 1858, he had made considerable progress in developing the inner harbor. A town had been laid out at New San Pedro, later called Wilmington, and work was well under way on wharves and warehouses. Married to the lovely Rebecca Sanford, he was already planning the stately home that was to become the showplace of Southern California.

Taking advantage of every business opportunity, Banning had built a successful forwarding and commission business. He held a monopoly on government contracts for transporting army supplies to both Fort Tejon and Fort Yuma. When it was announced that an army post would be established at Wilmington, he secured the contract for construction of the barracks.

Speed was extremely important, since with the firing on Fort Sumter in April of 1861, the Civil War had begun. Banning met the challenge. Soon Drum Barracks, named after Adjutant-General Richard C. Drum, commander of the post, was completed, and several thousand soldiers were stationed there. Naturally, the flourishing port at Wilmington became even more prosperous.

Among the many products handled by the Banning firm were large quantities of whale oil. In one week, whalers brought in more than two hundred barrels. When lumber began to replace adobe as a building material, Phineas took immediate steps to corner the new market. He advertised, "With accustomed promptness . . . the undersigned has received 100,000 feet of redwood lumber . . . also shortly to arrive 300,000 feet assorted Oregon lumber."

Banning, "the Irrepressible," never missed an opportunity to enlarge his enterprises, but he didn't forget his friends. During the drought he did what he could to help. Having obtained two enormous kettles at a cost of 1600 dollars, he contracted with his neighbors, Stearns, Temple and José Sepúlveda, to buy their cattle. These he "stewed up" for sale to the army. Processing as many as 200 cattle a day, he continued as long as the animals had any meat on their bones.

Throughout the deep depression of the drought years, Banning's prosperity stood out in marked contrast to the rest of Southern California. His energy and ingenuity never flagged. In addition to his brisk business with the army, he became chief supplier and shipper for extensive mining operations covering an area from San Gabriel to the Owens River Valley. Next he turned his attention to a daring new undertaking.

For several years he had been interested in the possibilities of oil in Southern California. Quietly he had been buying land which he considered promising. This included his purchase of one-fifth of the Rancho de los Palos Verdes from Pablo Pryor.

In January, 1865, ready to launch his new enterprise, he organized the Pioneer Oil Company. Certificate of incorporation was for 25 years. Five thousand shares of stock were issued at a par value of $300 each. The company owned property in San Fernando Valley and on the Rancho San Pasqual, as well as in los Palos Verdes. Plans were under way to bore wells as soon as necessary machinery could be obtained.

Banning was not completely immune to problems caused by the water shortage. Powerful steam pumps produced enough water from his wells to keep Wilmington reasonably supplied, but he was concerned about the hundreds of acres he had planted in orchards and grains. With the "accustomed promptness" for which he was famed, Phineas conceived a solution—the boring of deep, artesian wells.

A large-scale project was undertaken and, as far away as San Francisco, newspapers followed the experiment with avid interest. As usual, Banning was successful. While all his wells didn't come in, he obtained sufficient water to save his precious orchards.

Now it was time to bring to fruition his long-cherished dream of a home in keeping with his position in the community. Early the prior year, 1864, he had ordered the materials for the spacious colonial mansion. From all over the world they were assembled, including delicately veined Italian marble and exquisitely colored Belgian glass. Framed in the lovely fruit trees, the residence rose, the finest south of San Francisco.

As soon as Phineas could cajole the harried workmen into putting on the finishing touches and persuade his wife that the house was ready, he scheduled a full-scale "regale," as he called it. The memorable occasion was a dramatic moment in the history of Southern California. Standing in the elegant entrance hall, Phineas Banning, forerunner of a new aristocracy, welcomed the foremost representatives of an era now ending.

Among the first to arrive was the venerable Abel Stearns, once proud owner of El Palacio. With his customary dignity and courtly manner, he, and the lovely Arcadia, admired the luxurious appointments. In Stearns' regal bearing there was no hint of the fact that he was about to lose the Rancho Los Alamitos in a Sheriff's sale following a mortgage foreclosure.

Ascending the long, graceful staircase were the beautifully attired Doñas Rafaela Temple and Cesaria Sepúlveda. Their charming chatter hid the desperation in their hearts. Soon Doña Rafaela would have to leave her beloved hacienda and the 27,000 acres of land, which had been in her family since the grant given to Manual Nieto in 1784. And Cesaria knew it was only a question of time before José would have to give up his struggle to retain what was left to him of the Rancho de los Palos Verdes.

After a sumptuous dinner served in a room brilliantly lighted by another of Phineas' inventions, a refined oil made from turpentine, the men repaired to the library. Conversation centered about the events of the day. Naturally, the drought was a major topic of discussion.

So was an outfit by the name of Flint and Bixby, reported to have a highly profitable sheep business in Monterey County. Representatives of the firm had been south attempting to negotiate for purchase of range land. Apparently they had run into considerable resistance on the part of ranch owners.

As Abel Stearns' eyes met those of his old friend, Juan Temple, he raised his eyebrows. But both men kept their silence. Temple knew that Stearns was having a great deal of trouble meeting the terms of the $20,000 mortgage he had taken on Los Alamitos to finance building of the Arcadia Block, near the Plaza in Los Angeles. And, of course, Stearns knew about Temple's plans to sell his land for $20,000 and move to San Francisco.

Leaning against the elaborately carved mantlepiece, Banning, ebullient and assured, tried to raise the spirits of the group. He told them of his plans for the future of Los Angeles and the port, including his belief that railroads would soon span the continent. His optimism fell on deaf ears. The men to whom he was talking would not share in his triumphs.

Phineas now suggested that they join the ladies, and the festivities continued until well after midnight. Finally, the affair was over. As José and Cesaria were leaving, Banning took Sepúlveda aside.

"You've heard about my venture into oil, I suppose."

José nodded and laughed, then said smoothly, "Of course, my friend. You are to be congratulated. I wish you much success."

Phineas winced. Then, with obvious effort, continued.

"My partners in the company . . . I want you to know, for myself, I would not do this. They feel that the interests of the various owners of the Rancho Palos Verdes are not clear. They hold that a partition of the property is necessary for us to use our part."

José's strained face flushed darkly, but he maintained his composure, waiting for Banning to go on.

Phineas swallowed hard. "José, you must understand. I have to do this. I'm bringing suit for a partition of the Rancho."

José's brief laugh held a bitter tinge.

"I understand, of course," he said coldly. "And now, I must beg to be excused. My wife is waiting for me."

With a small courtly bow, he withdrew.

The judgment which Banning brought before the district court on

March 30, 1865, was the first of six partition suits and 78 lawsuits involving the Rancho de los Palos Verdes between that year and 1880.

When Flint, Bixby and Company purchased Los Cerritos from Juan Temple in 1866, the Bixbys entered Los Angeles County to stay. Llewellyn Bixby's younger brother, Jotham, was made manager of the property. It was not long before he acquired a taste for land of his own. Early in the 1870s he started buying interests in the Rancho de los Palos Verdes.

This was not difficult to do, as every year parcels of the land were offered for sale or mortgage sales threw portions of acreage on the market at public auction. Tax assessment rolls show that up to the fiscal year 1872-73, José Sepúlveda somehow managed to keep his one-fifth interest intact, but shortly thereafter his holdings started to fall apart.

Meanwhile several deaths changed the character of the Sepúlveda family. Diego died in 1869. He, too, had suffered losses during the drought but fared better than his brothers because of his involvement in harbor activities. He left his interest in the Rancho to his three surviving children: Aurelío, Román, and Rudecínda. During the litigation of the 1870s, they put up an effective battle for the land and salvaged over 4000 acres.

Before 1874, death also came to both Felipa and Cesaria Sepúlveda. Juan was remarried in 1868 to Susana Ruiz. For some time José was desolate.

For over thirty years he had come to count on the understanding and support of his beloved Cesaria. There was no one to share his anxiety when, in August of 1874, he was forced to mortgage one-tenth of the Rancho to the Farmers and Merchants Bank of Los Angeles, as security on a $1500 note. Though barely sixty, he felt like an old man, worn down by the burdens he had had to bear.

In his loneliness, it was not difficult for an attractive divorcee, Teodócia Gonzalez, to win his confidence and affection. On October 4, 1875, he deeded her "that part of the Rancho los Palos Verdes which interest has not yet been segregated and set apart to him but to which he is entitled as one of the original grantees . . . which interest he estimates to be worth $50,000."

The deed further stated that the property was given in "consideration of the love and affection which the party of the first part bears unto the party of the second part . . . and further consideration that the party of the second part has and does hereby agree to support said party of the first part during his natural life, providing for him at all times a suitable dwelling house, wholesome food and respectable clothing."

To such straits was the once proud Don José reduced.

In October, 1875, Teodócia and José were married. Less than a year later, she filed a complaint alleging that her husband "had been guilty of cruel and abusive conduct" and praying judgment for dissolution of the marriage and possession of the property which had been conveyed by the defendant.

This was only one of the many disillusionments suffered by José during the closing years of his life. Bit by bit he was fleeced of his property through delinquent taxes and mortgage foreclosures. In 1879, the Farmers and Merchants Bank foreclosed their mortgage, and Jotham Bixby bought the land at public auction for $2000. The children of Diego brought suit to claim their interest. Even his own children deserted him.

In February, 1881, José Sepúlveda died, a broken man, who never really understood what had happened to his heritage. The fact that the United States Government had finally issued a patent to Juan and José Sepúlveda for the Rancho de los Palos Verdes the prior June, meant nothing to him. Juan was appointed to represent his brother in the last days of litigation involving partition of the once vast estate.

By this time the Bixbys were firmly entrenched in Southern California. In addition to Los Cerritos, they had purchased the Rancho Los Alamitos from the heirs of Michael Reese, the money lender who had foreclosed on Abel Stearns. Jotham Bixby owned substantial interests in both of these properties, the future site of the city of Long Beach. In addition he had acquired over 17,000 acres of los Palos Verdes.

When the final decree was issued by the Superior Court, on September 25, 1882, Jotham received the lion's share of the Rancho de los Palos Verdes—half the original grant. This included all of what is today considered the Palos Verdes Peninsula, with the exception of San Pedro.

About a dozen persons shared in the partition of the remaining land. The heirs of Diego received the major portion of San Pedro; the rest went to A.W. Timms, the Town of San Pedro, and the old "Government Reserve" (now Fort MacArthur). Juan Sepúlveda was allowed to keep the tiny acreage deeded to him by his brothers, where he lived until his death in 1896.

8

A Great Seaport

AS THE ERA OF THE RANCHEROS was ending, the stage was set for a powerful new drama on the southeastern portion of the Palos Verdes Peninsula.

In this drama the principal players were the railroads. Both hero and villain of the piece was the Southern Pacific.

Out of this drama emerged the beginnings of the greatest man-made harbor in the world.

One man whose vast vision encompassed the future of that harbor was Phineas Banning. Neither derision nor denunciation could deflect him from his dream. To comprehend the magnitude of the undertaking required to bring this dream to fruition, it is necessary to visualize the harbor as it was in the 1860s.

Between the Banning wharves, at Wilmington, and the open sea was an enormous tide flat: 1300 acres of mud at low tide, and a lagoon with two to five feet of water at high tide. Through this delta ran a number of shallow channels, one of which led from the Main Channel through the area now known as the Turning Basin. It was along this route that Banning's lighters conveyed passengers and freight from ship to shore.

On the seaward side of the delta a large sand bar, named Rattlesnake Island, because of the reptiles which abounded there, formed a barrier.

Later this became the nucleus of the Terminal Island District. To the south, about where the United States Immigration Station is now located, was the rocky formation, rising from forty to fifty feet above water, which was called Dead Man's Island.

The width of the Main Channel at Dead Man's Island was 400 feet and, sometimes at low tide, the depth was only eighteen inches. It is not difficult to see why ships were unable to enter the Inner Harbor. To compound the problem, the Outer Harbor was merely an open roadstead, providing no natural protection from the sea.

Phineas Banning's plan for development of the port hinged upon the accomplishment of two objectives: dredging the Main Channel and constructing a breakwater, and bringing a railroad to the harbor.

So strong was his belief in the importance of a good seaport for Los Angeles that the prospect of losing his lucrative lighterage business did not deter him. Aware that federal appropriations would be required for the harbor improvement project, he used all his persuasiveness to prepare the way with influential contacts in Washington. At the same time, he never stopped trying to convince people that the future of Southern California was tied up with the railroads.

In 1866 Banning, then a State Senator, introduced a bill into the California State Legislature providing for a railroad from Los Angeles to the harbor. It passed without difficulty, but firing the Angelenos with enthusiasm "was like steaming up a cold locomotive with a candle under the crownsheet." Many saw the subsidies required as paving the road to bankruptcy. Holders of the large ranchos, already facing ruin, thought only of increased assessments. Men with vested interests, like Tomlinson of San Pedro, knew that the railroad would put an end to the stage business.

Two years later Banning tried again. By this time he had lined up support from some of the most powerful men in California, including ex-Governor Downey. The Legislature passed another bill, authorizing a bond issue of $150,000 by the County of Los Angeles and $75,000 by Los Angeles City for construction of a railroad between Los Angeles and Wilmington, subject to the will of the voters.

The Los Angeles and San Pedro Railroad Company was incorporated, with Banning, Downey, and Benito Wilson among those on the Board of Directors. These men lost no time in asking for a bond election. It was set for March 24th, allowing only two weeks for campaigning.

Feelings ran high. The opposition snarled that "the whole thing was just a scheme to make Los Angeles subservient to Banning's lighters

for all time." Banning countered with a promise "to carry the railroad
to deep water." The fight was brief but bitter, and the bonds passed by
a slim margin of 28 votes.

Now Banning determined to build and operate the railroad himself.
He arranged a partnership with Henry Tichenor, a lumber tycoon with
forests in Oregon and Northern California, who had experience in
building logging railroads. His Navarro River mills could supply redwood ties and bridge timbers, and he had a fleet of coastwise schooners
to transport them to San Pedro.

Bids started rolling in and the partners faced stiff competition. But
Banning was confident. He knew that his lighters would be essential
to integrated service on the railroad. The Banning-Tichenor offer was
to build and equip the railroad, 21 miles long, for $469,000, with Ban-
ning's steamers, barges, and docks thrown in. They got the contract.

On September 18th, all of Wilmington turned out for the Grand
Railroad Inaugural Ball at the Exchange Hotel. The next day Banning
turned the first shovelful of earth to break ground for his railroad. Eighteen hundred tons of iron were coming from Eastern and European mills,
and in Mendocino County Tichenor's loggers were turning out ties. The
job was under way.

It was a gigantic undertaking. In addition to railroad track, freight,
baggage, and passenger cars had to be built and depots constructed. Banning had to start from scratch and work with inexperienced help. But,
despite the constant carping of the Los Angeles *Star* about delays, he
completed the railroad better than two months before the deadline
stipulated in the contract.

On a bright, hot morning later in October, 1869, a crowd of more
than 1500 eager Angelenos assembled at the depot on the corner of Commercial and Alameda Streets. The spanking new engine, a trim eight-
wheeler named the "Los Angeles," stood steam up, waiting to haul them
on a gay excursion to Wilmington. The last tie, polished mountain laurel
with an engraved silver plate, presented by Wells, Fargo and Company,
was pounded home. The crowd cheered. Southern California's first
railroad was officially opened!

That same year two events significant to the future of the harbor
took place. In May, 1869, at a tiny dot on the map just east of the northern
tip of the Great Salt Lake, two railroads met. The Central Pacific and
the Union Pacific were joined and the nation spanned by a transcontinental railroad. Now the port at San Pedro Bay would have real competition from San Francisco.

At the same time the lobbying activities of Banning and his associates bore fruit, and a corps of army engineers came out from Washington to survey the possibilities of improving the Inner Harbor. They agreed that a breakwater between Rattlesnake and Dead Man's Islands would create a current in the Main Channel resulting in deepening to the point where ships of some size could enter. Accordingly, they submitted a report and cost estimate to Congress,

Shortly after completion of its transcontinental link, the Central Pacific acquired the Southern Pacific, a line running from San Francisco to Gilroy, with plans to extend it south and east. Soon there would be a railroad joining East and West through the southern part of the nation. When that happened, it was imperative for Los Angeles to be on the main line. The Los Angeles and San Pedro Railroad was a good beginning, but without an overland connection both Los Angeles and the harbor would atrophy.

Principal owners and promoters of the Central Pacific Railroad were Leland Stanford, Collis Huntington, Mark Hopkins and Charles Crocker. Stanford especially was friendly towards San Pedro, and Banning had been doing everything he could to interest the Big Four in development of the harbor area. Toward the close of 1870, a group of Southern Pacific engineers made a survey to determine if Los Angeles could be included in the projected route from Gilroy to the Colorado River.

They reported the idea to be impractical. A tunnel nearly 7000 feet long would have to be dug through the San Fernando Mountains, at a cost of approximately $2,500,000.

The population of Los Angeles was still small and preponderantly Mexican and, with the decline of the cattle industry, the economy was in a state of transition. A useful harbor was much more a dream than a reality. The Big Four decided that Los Angeles was not worth the gamble.

Banning stood up to this blow with his customary aplomb. He countered by announcing he would extend the Los Angeles and San Pedro Railroad across the Colorado to Prescott, Arizona, and connect with the Atlantic and Pacific Railroad from the East. Always ready to try daring innovations, he proposed to include a thirty-inch narrow gauge branch to the Owens Valley, where booming mines provided Los Angeles with a lucrative business.

But months passed and nothing further happened. It became painfully apparent that capital could not be raised to build the railroad. Somehow the Big Four would have to be wooed and won.

Meanwhile Banning was approaching accomplishment of the second objective of his plan for development of the harbor. On March 2, 1871, Congress voted an appropriation for construction of a rock jetty from the lower end of Rattlesnake Island to Dead Man's Island, closing the gaps in the sandbar between the two islands and creating a current which would dredge the Main Channel to a depth of at least ten feet. More importantly, this appropriation marked the beginning of allocation of federal money for the creation of a real harbor at San Pedro Bay. By October, 1871, 150 men were at work building the breakwater.

A new urgency possessed those who felt the need to persuade the Southern Pacific to reroute its railroad through Los Angeles. Every passing day of construction on the railroad made this possibility more remote. And still there were those who spluttered about the "railroad gang" whose schemes were merely to enrich themselves.

Early in May, 1872, a group gathered in the County Courthouse to hear Banning and Downey discuss strategy for bringing a railroad through Los Angeles. A committee was appointed, and Downey volunteered to go to San Francisco and have a chat with Leland Stanford. Three weeks later the committee received a letter. Stanford and Crocker were not uninterested. The Big Four would run the Southern Pacific through Los Angeles for a five per cent subsidy with no strings attached and the Los Angeles and San Pedro Railroad to boot.

The County Board of Supervisors agreed to submit the proposal to the electorate. Then the real fight began. Suddenly on August 25th, Colonel Thomas Scott, president of the Union Pacific, arrived at Wilmington. He had secured a franchise to build his Texas and Pacific Railroad to San Diego. He had a competitive offer to make. For the same five per cent subsidy, but without the Los Angeles and San Pedro Railroad thrown in, he would build the San Diego and Los Angeles Railroad, from Los Angeles to Anaheim and thence to the best point of junction with the Texas and Pacific. Both propositions were placed on the November ballot.

As election time drew near, political temperatures ran higher than ever before. Many believed that Los Angeles should "keep out of the clutches of the Southern Pacific people." Others felt that it was dangerous to alienate the Southern Pacific, a powerful corporation which "if irked at a community could leave it to die on the vine while a railroad-created rival boomed." Still others were dead set against any kind of subsidies to railroads.

All three sides campaigned vigorously. There were outdoor and indoor meetings, blazing bonfires, torchlight parades, and endless

Dedication of "the drugstore building," the Plaza's first business edifice, September 13, 1925.
(Courtesy Palos Verdes Library District, Local History Room)

Phillips Barn and Three 8-Horse Teams, across from the present-day Botanic Garden. *(Courtesy Palos Verdes Library District, Local History Room)*

La Venta Inn, early 1920s. Designed in the tradition of a Spanish seaside hostelry by Walter Swindell Davis, the inn was first used by the Palos Verdes Project to entertain prospective buyers of property. *(Courtesy Palos Verdes Library District, Local History Room)*

The "Cottage" built by Frank A. Vanderlip, Sr., in 1916. *(Photo by William Webb)*

Frederick Law Olmsted transformed the north entrance to Palos Verdes Estates into an all-year garden of radiant bloom, 1925. Gardner Building in the background. *(Courtesy Palos Verdes Library District, Local History Room)*

Residence of Frederick Law Olmsted in left foreground; embryonic business district in background, 1925. *(Courtesy Palos Verdes Library District, Local History Room)*

Palos Verdes was "way out in the country" in 1925. Left center, the Malaga Cove Plaza business district begins with the Gardner Building. *(Courtesy Palos Verdes Library District, Local History Room)*

Charles H. Cheney home. *(Courtesy Palos Verdes Library District, Local History Room)*

The Palos Verdes Library. Designed by Myron Hunt and landscaped by
Frederick Law Olmsted, the stately Spanish building was completed in 1930.
It adjoins Farnham Martin Park, dedicated to the memory of the man who
was Superintendent of Parks for the Palos Verdes Project. *(Photo by William Webb)*

Home of J.J. Haggerty, later became the Neighborhood Church.
(Courtesy Palos Verdes Library District, Local History Room)

128

The "Villetta," built in
1924, as a guesthouse, by
Frank A. Vanderlip, Sr.
(Photo by William Webb)

The Farmstead, a replica of a Tuscany farmhouse of the early Renaissance
period. *(Photo by William Webb)*

A flight of 268 stone steps soars from the "Villetta" to a
lookout point and marble temple.
(Photo by William Webb)

Wreck of the Greek freighter, *Dominator*, at the base of Rocky Point; fragments may still be seen at low tide, testimony to the treacherous reefs.
(Photo by William Webb)

The Villa Francesca, built by Harry Benedict, in 1926.
(Photo by William Webb)

speeches. When the great day came, the Southern Pacific proposal won by a tremendous majority: 1896 to 99 in the County and 1093 to 14 in the City.

That Angelenos made a wise choice cannot be denied. The Texas and Pacific never got to San Diego. But the price Los Angeles paid for its place on a transcontinental railroad was far greater than it appeared to be at the time.

Through its acquisition of the Los Angeles and San Pedro Railroad, the Southern Pacific gained a foothold in the harbor area which gave it enormous influence upon developments in the next two decades, culminating in the fight for a free harbor. The series of events, which slowly but inexorably led up to this fight, started with arrival upon the scene of Senator John P. Jones in December of 1874.

The Senator from Nevada had made a fortune in the Comstock Lode and owned extensive interests in the mines of Owens Valley. Now he wanted to get aboard the railroad bandwagon. He reconnoitered an area then known as "Shoo Fly," which was originally the Rancho San Vicente y Santa Monica. It had been purchased a couple of years before by Colonel R.S. Baker, husband of the widowed Arcadia Stearns. The large expanse of ocean frontage immediately appealed to Senator Jones. Promptly he made a deal, buying a three-fourths interest in the ranch and entering into partnership with Baker to build a railroad.

The Los Angeles and Independence Railroad was incorporated, and it was announced that the road would first be built from Santa Monica to Los Angeles, then extended to the Owens Valley and on beyond to Nevada. This would provide a direct line from the Senator's mining interests to the sea. Early in 1875 construction was under way on the railroad and on a 1700-foot wharf.

The new line found favor with many people nettled by the Southern Pacific's monopoly of port facilities and control of freight rates, which they kept at the level of "all the traffic would bear." A second source of irritation was the high charge of lighterage. Santa Monica had the advantage of an open harbor, but on the other hand it offered no protection from storms and could only be used in calm weather. In Washington Senator Jones started lobbying for a breakwater for his facility.

Meanwhile Banning was making every effort to secure more federal money for the harbor at San Pedro. Dredging and work on the breakwater continued and proved quite effective. Small steamers could make their way through the entrance channel. But large vessels still could not enter and there was no protected Outer Harbor.

Those who wanted to criticize also found fuel for their fuming in the slowness of construction of the Southern Pacific's road to Los Angeles. Some Cassandras cried that even if a tunnel through the San Fernando Mountains were completed, it would cave in with the first heavy rains. To this Leland Stanford retorted, "It is too damned dry in Southern California for any such catastrophe."

Eighteen hundred seventy-five was a year of triumph for Senator Jones. In the summer his wharf was completed, and on October 17th the first train on the Los Angeles and Independence Railroad ran from Santa Monica to Los Angeles. By December a real estate boom had gotten underway and Santa Monica had a thousand residents. Soon many steamers were stopping at the wharf and much freight began to move on the new railroad.

Then suddenly the Southern Pacific went into action. They dropped freight rates between Wilmington and Los Angeles from $5 a ton to $2.50. Of course Senator Jones had to match their price. Several months later Southern Pacific rates dropped to $1 a ton and passenger fares to 50 cents. Again the Senator was forced to meet the competition. It was now a life and death struggle, and both sides knew it.

In September, 1876, at a gala ceremony in Soledad Canyon, attended by dignitaries from both San Francisco and Los Angeles, a solid gold spike was driven home uniting the two cities by rail. Los Angeles had its transcontinental railroad, and Banning's dream of rail service between San Pedro Harbor and the East had become a reality.

By this time the Southern Pacific's rate war was beginning to tell on Senator Jones. There were rumors that he was trying to sell the Los Angeles and Independence Railroad and had offered it to Los Angeles County. But it was a year of drought and depression, and there was no money in government coffers for the purchase of railroads. Besides, it would be dangerous to incur the displeasure of the Big Four.

Early in 1877, Stanford visited Santa Monica with a corps of engineers, and in June the Southern Pacific moved in for the kill. They bought the Senator's railroad for about half of what it had cost to build. Promptly original rates were restored on both roads, the wharf at Santa Monica was declared unsafe and competition ended.

Ironically, the move which gave the Southern Pacific back its monopoly of port facilities appeared to favor San Pedro but later proved the basis on which that harbor was almost lost to the people of Southern California. For the time being, however, the Big Four concentrated attention on the San Pedro facility.

In 1881 they secured a right-of-way acrosss the Wilmington Lagoon and along a strip of land, two hundred feet wide, on the west side of the Main Channel. They then extended the Los Angeles and San Pedro Railroad on piling across the lagoon, between what later became the East and West Basins, to the vicinity of Timms' Point. Now freight and passenger trains could reach deep water. San Pedro's star was ascending.

It was time to tackle the problem of the Outer Harbor. During the 1880s, Los Angeles experienced a period of great growth. Population of the city increased from 15,000 to over 50,000. Real estate values soared and industries took root. Harbor tonnage increased from 50,000 tons in 1871 to 450,000 tons in 1888. Aware of the acute need for a deepwater harbor, business interests of Los Angeles and San Pedro started a movement for a breakwater easterly from Point Fermin.

The project found a powerful champion in the newly formed Los Angeles Chamber of Commerce. Leland Stanford, then president of the Southern Pacific, gave it his support. Phineas Banning had died in 1885, but it looked as if his second great dream was about to be accomplished.

Then several forces converged which almost shattered the future of San Pedro Harbor. The first of these was the appearance of two new railroads on the Southern California scene.

The Santa Fe, which had been pushing westward for a number of years, completed its road from the Mojave Desert to San Diego. It also built a branch line from Colton through Los Angeles to Redondo Beach. Although Redondo had no harbor, a submarine canyon came close to its shore. The Santa Fe constructed a wharf along the edge of the canyon, and ships were able to unload there except in very rough weather. A considerable commerce developed, especially in lumber. The Southern Pacific's monopoly was threatened a bit.

At about the same time, a more dangerous rival to the Southern Pacific appeared. A group of Saint Louis capitalists formed a corporation called the Los Angeles Terminal Railway. The company purchased Rattlesnake Island and built a railroad from Los Angeles to Long Beach, then westward along the shore of the island to a terminus on the Main Channel across from the town of San Pedro. There they constructed a wharf. The Los Angeles Terminal Railway owned acres of ocean frontage and an excellent location for ships to land. The Southern Pacific faced serious competition.

Meanwhile Congress had passed a bill establishing a board of engineers to survey the coast from Point Dume to Capistrano in order to ascertain the best location for a deepwater harbor. At this critical moment in the history of San Pedro Harbor, an event took place which threatened to put an end to its development. Collis P. Huntington replaced Leland Stanford as President of the Southern Pacific Railroad.

Annoyed by the encroachment of competition, Huntington decided that the deepwater harbor should be located at Santa Monica where he had complete control. Within a few months of his election to its presidency, the Southern Pacific began construction of an extension of the Los Angeles and Independence Railroad to a point two miles north of the town of Santa Monica. There work was started on a 4300-foot wharf.

The following year, 1891, the governor's survey board made its report to Congress, favoring San Pedro and recommending an appropriation of three million dollars for harbor construction. It was assumed that location of the harbor was settled. When Congress met, Angelenos' hopes ran high for an immediate appropriation by the Committee on Commerce. But they had failed to reckon on the influence of Collis Huntington.

A close friend of Huntington, Senator Frye from Maine was a member of the Commerce Committee. During the debate, he produced a telegram from William Hood, Chief of Engineers for the Southern Pacific. It stated that the holding ground at San Pedro Bay was rock and that it would be impossible to drive piles into this hard bottom. Wielding the Hood telegram, Frye managed to get the appropriation thrown out of committee.

It is revealing to note that no public record was made of this telegram. Four years later, Hood testified that the San Pedro holding ground was free from rock. The telegram was a warning of the lengths to which Huntington would go to protect his interests. It proved to be the opening gun of an eight-year fight between the Southern Pacific and the people of Los Angeles, later known at "The Free Harbor Contest."

A second board of engineers, the "Craighill Board," was appointed by Congress once again to investigate the need for a deepwater harbor and the best location for it. Its report, filed in October, 1892, stated that such a harbor was "of high national importance," and that "the location at San Pedro is decidedly the best as regards adaptability for construction and maintenance." The question appeared surely to be settled.

The Los Angeles Chamber of Commerce sent a special delegation to Washington to try to get an appropriation through Congress. The measure never got out of the Committee on Commerce, of which Senator Frye was chairman. Now, public opinion became divided.

Merchants felt threatened. They knew the Southern Pacific could be a powerful friend or foe. It could give rebates and fast service to its favorites. It could also destroy the business of a shipper who didn't go along with its program. Many Angelenos said that it made little difference whether the harbor was located at Santa Monica or San Pedro. Others contended that a Santa Monica location would mean a "monopoly harbor" as the Southern Pacific owned all the land along the shore there.

By 1893, the Southern Pacific's railroad extension and wharf at Santa Monica were in operation, and much business was transferring there from San Pedro. People viewed the activities of Collis Huntington with increasing alarm, especially when he flatly stated to representatives of the Los Angeles Chamber of Commerce, "I do not find it to my advantage to have this harbor built at San Pedro, and I shall be compelled to oppose all efforts that you or others make to secure appropriations for that site. On the other hand, the Santa Monica location will suit me perfectly, and if you folks will get in and work for that, you will find me on your side."

It began to look as if the question were not Santa Monica or San Pedro, but Santa Monica or nothing. Despite its reputation as the "octopus" in Northern California, many people supported the Southen Pacific. They felt that it was an efficient operation and had contributed greatly to the prosperity of Southern California. The fight grew hotter and hotter.

On April 7, 1894, the Los Angeles Chamber of Commerce passed a resolution calling for a vote of the entire membership on whether they favored San Pedro or Santa Monica as the site for a deepwater harbor. During the week's interval before the vote was taken, a spirited campaign was waged. Thundering editorials appeared in the Los Angeles *Times* supporting San Pedro, while the Los Angeles *Express* and the Los Angeles *Herald* countered with barrages backing Santa Monica. When the votes were in, they stood 328 to 131 in favor of San Pedro.

With the appointment of California's Senator Stephen M. White to the Committee on Commerce, another attempt was made to secure an appropriation for San Pedro. But Collis Huntington, true to his threat, kept the committee from taking any action.

Now, not only Southern California but the whole nation was indignant. Eastern newspapers took up the cry. The New York *World* demanded, "is this a government by the people, for the people, or a government by Mr. Huntington, for Mr. Huntington?"

Almost two years of bickering and political maneuvering ensued. Then the bomb exploded. In 1896, a year in which supposedly the United

States Treasury was drained of money and a strict economy program was in force, $3,000,000 was voted by the Committee on Commerce for construction of a breakwater at Santa Monica!

Desperately, Senator White attempted to divert the appropriation to San Pedro but failed. As a last resort, he introduced an amendment to the bill, stipulating that a new commission be appointed to investigate the harbor question and that the allocation of the appropriation be settled by its recommendation. Five days of fierce debate on the floor of the Senate followed. Finally Senator White's repeated taunt that Senator Frye did not dare refer the question to an unprejudiced board won his case. The amendment was passed.

The new board of engineers, known as the "Walker Board," reported unequivocally in favor of San Pedro, but still the fight was not over. For months, Secretary of War Alger, a friend of Huntington, held up the report and recommendation for appropriations. During this time, Huntington attempted to introduce another bill into Congress, which would have nullified the effect of the report. Not until February, 1898, were bids opened for construction of the San Pedro breakwater, and it was April, 1899, when the first bargeload of rock was dropped on the site.

At last the fight for a free harbor had been won.

The next important step in harbor development was the acquisition by Los Angeles of the famous "shoestring strip." In 1906, the city acquired a strip of land, half a mile wide, extending from Slauson Avenue to a point within a mile of tidewater on what later became the West Basin. It then passed an ordinance establishing the Los Angeles Harbor Commission.

One of the first concerns of the commission was the fixing of harbor lines. This required authorization by Congress. Frank Flint, then United States Senator from California, obtained passage of the necessary bill, and the Secretary of War appointed a board of three engineers.

The task of the Harbor Line Board was not easy. It had to preserve a balance between reclaimed land and water so that the ebb and flow of the tides would keep the channels free of debris and silt. Space had to be provided for warehouses, rail terminals, roads, and other port accessories. Deepwater areas had to be planned to handle large oceangoing ships. Bulkhead and pier lines had to be placed. When the work of the board was completed, the plan for the harbor was substantially as it appears today.

Implementation of the plan involved a fresh set of problems. Improvement of the Inner Harbor required the dredging of channels to the north of the entrance at Dead Man's Island to a depth of thirty feet. Thus would be created the Turning Basin at the head of the Main Channel, with a lateral to the east leading to the East Basin and another lateral extending under the Southern Pacific Railroad trestle to the West Basin.

The first problem encountered was that a large portion of the tidelands in the Wilmington Lagoon was owned by private interests, principally the Banning heirs and the Southern Pacific. As the City of Los Angeles held no claim to the area, and only the State Attorney General had authority to question the legality of the private claims, the City Council requested permission to file suits in the name of the State. This was granted, and suits were entered to invalidate eleven different tideland claims, including the Southern Pacific's right-of-way.

While the tideland litigation was pending, the second major obstacle to harbor improvement was attacked. The City of Los Angeles could not spend municipal funds on a harbor outside of its boundaries. Annexation of Wilmington and San Pedro appeared to be the only answer. With the acquisition of the "shoestring strip," these cities had been made contiguous territory; thereby satisfying one legal requirement for annexation. But there was no legal provision for one incorporated city to annex another.

In January, 1909, a bill was introduced into the State Legislature providing for consolidation of incorporated cities. It passed, despite bitter opposition from corporations with tideland claims and citizens of the harbor cities who resented being taken over by Los Angeles. Now, the election for consolidation had to be engineered.

This required careful planning. Each municipality was asked to name a consolidation committee. These three committees framed the consolidation agreement, known as the "bill of rights," which governed the relations of the three communities for a generation.

Representatives of the harbor cities drove a hard bargain. Among the many pledges Los Angeles was required to make was that it spend at least $10,000,000 on harbor improvements within ten years, and that a bond election be called immediately after consolidation to vote the first $3,000,000. When the consolidation elections were held, early in August, 1909, they carried by large majorities.

The southeastern portion of the Palos Verdes Peninsula was now a part of the City of Los Angeles, and the Port of Los Angeles had come into being.

The tideland litigation ended in victory for the City of Los Angeles. In 1911, it received the gift of tide and submerged lands from the State of California, and by 1912 the promised $3,000,000 worth of improvement bonds had been voted. That same year the first section of the federally financed breakwater was completed. Subsequent additions brought the breakwater to a length of nine miles, with a 2100-foot-wide entrance at Angel's Gate.

In the aftermath of World War I, a vigorous upsurge of commercial activity came to the Port of Los Angeles. By 1923, there were four shipbuilding yards in the harbor, and both the lumber and petroleum industries relied heavily on its facilities. In a single year, 1928, the harbor handled over 25 million tons of cargo. To accommodate the larger, oil-burning steamers, with increased cargo capacity, channels were widened and deepened. In addition, wharves and storage areas were enlarged, and loading equipment modernized. At the same time, a thriving canning industry evolved, as thousands of fishermen were attracted by rich albacore and abalone fields.

During the 1930s, there was a hiatus in development, as the Great Depression weakened the maritime industry. But with the advent of World War II, the long-idle shipyards were reactivated, and the post-war boom brought a new impetus to commercial traffic in the harbor. Leading the way was the petroleum industry, as Americans became increasingly dependent on the automobile. To accommodate the giant tankers, the Harbor Commission responded with a stepped-up program of construction and expansion. Then, in the 1960s, revolutionary shipping techniques demanded not only larger facilities but new cargo-handling systems. The special needs of containerships, supertankers, and auto carriers initiated the most aggressive building program the Port of Los Angeles had undertaken since the 1920s. By 1965, the harbor development represented a total investment of almost $200,000,000. Of this amount, only $50,000,000 contributed by the Federal Government was not covered by harbor revenues. The Port is now entirely self-sustaining, relying on its own earnings and bonds for capital funds.

The present-day Port of Los Angeles comprises a 7000-acre harbor complex that includes 28 miles of waterfront, 200 acres of shed and warehouse space, terminals for all types of commodities, and 23 huge container cranes. Some 100,000 tons of cargo pass over its wharves each day, as the Port provides a gateway for the 70 steamship lines serving inland markets from the Pacific Basin. But despite its status as one of the greatest seaports in the world, it does not rest on its laurels. Plans are underway for further expansion and improvement, with about $100 million per year earmarked for over 50 capital development projects.

Moreover, concern for the enhancement of recreational facilities has kept pace with the growth of commercial operations. Passenger cruise terminals have been opened, beaches and parks are immaculately maintained, and the 370-acre West Channel/Cabrillo Beach Recreational Complex, which includes a 1150-slip marina, is currently under construction.

Within the scant space of 130 years, miracles of engineering have transformed the mudflats of San Pedro Harbor into the West Coast's "Gateway to the World." Phineas Banning's dream of a free port for Los Angeles has emerged as a world-renowned center of commerce, industry, and navigation. Proudly it bears the name WORLDPORT/PORT OF LOS ANGELES, as it meets the needs of today and prepares for the demands of tomorrow.

9

An Awakening in Paradise

AT THE CLOSE OF THE 19TH CENTURY, while portentous events were taking place in the San Pedro portion of the Peninsula, the Palos Verdes Hills lay dormant.

Uninhabited except for sheepherders, the vast lonely land was without a tree, fence or cultivated plot of ground. Its owner, Jotham Bixby, lived at Los Cerritos and had extensive land holdings in several Southern California counties. It was not surprising that for him the high mesas and sweeping terraces of the great headland held little interest other than as range country for his cattle and sheep.

A glimpse of what Los Palos Verdes was like at the time is provided by Jotham's neice, Sarah Bixby Smith, in her book, *Adobe Days*.

We had cattle on both the Alamitos and the Cerritos but the greater range was the Palos Verdes. Those were the exciting mornings when, at dawn, the men and boys started off for the roundup on the hills beyond Wilmington, Uncle Jotham and father in the single buggy with two strong horses that would take them up and down the ravines and over the hills where no roads were. I have been told that sometimes they would ride along a hillside where the slant was so steep that in order to prevent the carriage from tipping over men on horseback would fasten their reatas to the upper side and ride above them.

But then as always there were men for whom the wild raw beauty of the Peninsula held a magnetic appeal. Such a man was Harry Phillips. In 1887, he came to San Pedro from Julian, bringing his bride of a few months. Applying his experience as a mining engineer in the mountains back of San Diego, he roamed the Palos Verdes Hills, locating the hidden springs in deep-cleft canyons. Before long he became an authority on water sources on the Bixby property.

When in 1894 Jotham Bixby's son, George, who inherited the Peninsula portion of his father's estate, wanted a ranch manager, he selected Phillips. He charged him with responsibility for improving the productivity of the steep and rocky shoreland. Phillips did an excellent job.

He brought to the Peninsula knowledge, imagination and a love of the land. First he began upgrading the Bixby stock, a mongrel lot including some descendents of the desiccated Sepúlveda herds. He introduced thoroughbred Hereford bulls and sold off the inferior stock for beef. In a few years, he had developed 2000 fine head of cattle.

One of his longest lasting contributions was the institution of farming operations. Early in the 1900s he persuaded the Japanese to rent land at $10 an acre and cultivate vegetables. Beans, peas and tomatoes were the principal crops, and the acreage was on the moist southern slopes, with a concentration around Portuguese Bend. Soon there were forty families working the land. Kumekichi Ishibashi was one of the first tenants, and his son, Masaichi, was still farming in the same area in the 1960s.

The first house that Harry Phillips built for his family was a simple wood structure with adjoining corral, just east of the present Rolling Hills city hall and gate house. To this he brought his wife and four children. His eldest son, Harry Phillips, Jr., wistfully recalled, "When I was a kid, that country was paradise."

The Phillips family raised barley for hay and grain. Other Caucasian families joined them, renting suitable land on the crest of the hills and the northeastern slopes. Soft, silvery fields of grain began to cover the once barren land. Trees began to appear. Phillips planted a mass of seedlings along the north border of the ranch, which grew into Palos Verdes Estates' proud eucalyptus grove.

The annual springtime roundup was a thrilling time. In the spring of 1911, Phillips had 18 vaqueros. Each rode his cow horse, which knew almost as much about roping and dragging a calf as the rider. Seven-year-old Llewellyn Phillips, "whose legs did not reach halfway down his pony's sides, roped and brought in alone and unaided 15 calves in three hours' time."

There were hardships as well as thrills in those early days. Gas and electricity were unthought-of-luxuries. Coyotes howled around the houses at night. Water was a continuing cause for concern. Not only did crops depend upon rainfall, but it was also caught in tubs for drinking purposes. Phillips partially alleviated the problem by developing several wells from springs.

One of these was located in Blackwater Canyon, where Phillips built the second home for his family. This was a four-bedroom house slightly to the northeast of the present intersection of Palos Verdes Drive North and Rolling Hills Road. It was called "The Farmery," a colloquial English term that included both the farmhouse and outbuildings. Among the latter was the "Red Barn," long a familiar Peninsula landmark. Today a plaque marks the area where the Phillips family spent so many happy years.

A wonderful camaraderie existed among the first families of the Peninsula. Grain farmers and vegetable gardeners, Caucasian and Japanese, they were all close friends sharing their crops and daily lives. "Frugal, dependable, generous, industrious," they were part of the land. But their idyll was soon ended.

The beauty of the place, which had seeped into their bones, brought others with different ideas of what to do with the terraced land. The last roundup was held in 1912 and by the early 1920s, the Phillips family as well as many of the tenant farmers had left. The advent of the entrepreneurs was underway.

Early in 1913, Bixby had decided to sell 16,000 acres of Los Palos Verdes; all of what he owned of the Peninsula, except for about 1000 acres in what is now Harbor City. His purchaser was a man by the name of Walter Fundenburg, who agreed to pay $1,500,000. The terms were $600,000 in cash and the balance in one year. Mr. Fundenburg was unable to raise sufficient capital and assigned the property to the real estate firm of Schader and Adams. They, too, were unable to meet the terms of the agreement. Bixby foreclosed the mortgage, and the case was thrown into court.

After extended litigation, a compromise decree was issued allowing Schader and Adams 90 days to complete the purchase. Immediately, Mr. Schader left for New York to see if he could find a buyer and salvage the money which had been invested. He was able to interest Frank A. Vanderlip, then President of the National City Bank of New York.

Mr. Vanderlip had never seen the Palos Verdes Peninsula, but he was aware of its strategic location and potential for development. Quickly he raised the required capital and organized a syndicate to develop the property. The deal was consummated in November of 1913.

First developers of the Peninsula were some fifty millionaires, including representatives from such national powerhouses as J.P. Morgan and Company, Bankers' Trust Company of New York, and the Chesapeake and Ohio Railroad. Their plans were nothing short of munificent. By the middle of July, 1914, preliminary sketches had been submitted to them by the noted architects, Howard Shaw of Chicago and Myron Hunt of Los Angeles, and the famed Massachusetts landscape engineering firm of Frederick Law Olmsted.

A magnificent country club was to be erected on the bluffs above Portuguese Bend, comprising 150 guest rooms, numerous dining and community rooms, as well as "card rooms, reading rooms, writing rooms, and locker rooms." The plans provided for a swimming pool 60 by 120 feet in dimensions, golf links, tennis courts, polo grounds, and a yacht club with concrete pier. Sketches for the main building, which was to be known as "Los Palos Verdes Country Club," showed an enormous rambling structure of mission design, with a multitude of towers, gables and arcades.

Plans of the syndicate were not limited to the club; they included development of the entire 16,000 acres into the "most fashionable and exclusive residence colony" in the nation. The well-known engineering firm of Koebig and Koebig made an extensive contour survey of the ranch. More than 100 miles of roads were laid out and a wide highway was planned to follow around the 14 miles of shoreline.

Three "model villages" were projected. It was stated that, "in each village the architecture of every building, from the business blocks to the humblest cottages, will be regulated, it being the intention of the syndicate to create towns having all the charm of some places that so delight tourists traveling in certain rural districts of Germany and England. These villages will constitute the shopping points for the colonists, making their domain a small principality to itself."

The dramatic dreams of Mr. Vanderlip and his associates were not destined for immediate fulfillment. By 1916 Frank Vanderlip had demonstrated his devotion to the compelling beauty of the Peninsula by establishing a summer home on the slopes above Portuguese Bend. Building materials and furniture had to be brought from San Pedro on a narrow, rutted road to accomplish the undertaking. It was a beginning, but for seven years "the Cottage," as it was called, stood as the only visible fruition of the first "Palos Verdes Project."

With the entrance of the United States into the First World War, men's minds were occupied with matters other than the establishment of elaborate country estates. By the time the Armistice came, members of the syndicate had lost interest. Then the Palos Verdes property came to the attention of an experienced real estate promoter.

E.G. Lewis was the highly imaginative but quixotic originator of two sensational real estate developments: Universal City in St. Louis, and Atascadero in San Luis Obispo County, California. He was also the founder, and chief executive, of an organization known as The Commonwealth. This organization was based on some rather unusual propositions.

Its purpose, according to Mr. Lewis, was to consider "brains and effort as capital and on exactly the same footing as money." Employees of The Commonwealth were considered to have invested capital in an amount on which six per cent annual interest would be equivalent to their wages. During their employment, they were to "participate in one-third of the annual net incomes from all The Commonwealth enterprises," in addition to their wages, and to receive "credit for the total period of all employment on Brain-Capital account."

Capital members of The Commonwealth, of whom there were supposedly thousands throughout the United States, Canada, and Mexico, provided funds for Commonwealth enterprises. They were in "three grades," loaning respectively $100, $500, and $1000 on "Capital Reserve Notes." These notes matured in 26 years and bore an annual interest of 6 per cent. In addition, capital members were "entitled to a pro rata of one-third of all net incomes annually," for life!

In August of 1921, Mr. Lewis took an option to purchase the Palos Verdes property for $5,000,000, or $312 an acre. He proposed the building of a complete city, "under one general plan, and at one time," for an ultimate population of 200,000 people. He estimated the cost of the city, excepting the construction of private homes, at $30,000,000. The estimate included parklands, schools, public buildings, clubs, golf links, flying fields, a yacht harbor, 125 miles of paved boulevards, and trust funds of $5,000,000 for building loans and $4,000,000 for transportation facilities. He set the time for completion of the city at three years.

To finance the undertaking, an issue of trust indenture notes, equal to the $35,000,000 total cost of the project, was offered to the public for subscription on the basis of 10 per cent cash and the balance in thirty-six monthly payments with interest at 7 per cent per annum. The Title Insurance and Trust Company of Los Angeles was made trustee.

Under the terms of the trust indenture, a minimum underwriting subscription of $15,000,000 had to be secured or the project abandoned, the subscriptions canceled, and the money refunded to the subscribers. This amount was offered as convertible notes, giving the investors first and exclusive right to select property of a value equivalent to their subscription, at $312 an acre plus cost of improvements. According to Mr. Lewis, this portion of the underwriting was completed by May 31, 1922.

The balance of the issue, that is $20,000,000, was offered in non-convertible notes, representing equitable ownership in the remaining property. Holders of these notes were to ''receive 100 per cent from liquidation of assets, and then 90 per cent of all profits.'' Mr. Lewis, as fee for managing the project, was to receive the remaining 10 per cent of the profits, in addition to the 7 per cent of interest on deferred subscription payments, 5 per cent of the $35,000,000 underwriting at the time of its completion, and 5 per cent of the proceeds of sale or lease of the trust real property. A complicated arrangement, but one from which Lewis stood to make a good profit.

Of course as an employee of The Commnowealth, he would have to turn over all fees to that organization. Also the trust indenture agreement specified that not a dollar of the underwriting funds were to be spent for the expense of the underwriting, advertising, commissions, and fees paid to staff hired to plan the project. This was to be Mr. Lewis's contribution. By July, 1922, he stated that these expenses had amounted to approximately three-quarters of a million dollars.

He appealed to members of The Commonwealth for help in terms of personal loans to him. These were to be repaid in cash at the time the underwriting was completed, plus an amount of underwriting notes equal to the loans subscribed and paid for by Mr. Lewis, as a bonus. But if by any chance the underwriting campaign proved unsuccessful, the members' investment would be a total loss. Members advanced $600,000.

On January 17, 1923, Lewis announced that he had completed the preliminary part of the Palos Verdes promotion and was turning the project over to the Title Insurance and Trust Company. Then, like a bolt from the blue, the Title Insurance Company issued a letter to all subscribers, on February 7th, stating all the conditions of the trust indenture had not been fulfilled and therefore they could have their money back.

According to a reliable source, the Board of Directors of the Title Insurance Company for some time had been split in their feelings about the soundness of Lewis's handling of the project. When Stuart O'Melveny joined the company, "his presence on the board added another conservative voice, most welcome to President Allen." The Board voted to pull out of the project and return all cash received on the subscription notes.

Consternation hit the staff of the project. Frank Vanderlip was summoned from New York. He invited local subscribers to a mass meeting at which Lewis made an impassioned appeal to save the project. They were told that a new company was to be incorporated immediately, under the name of The Commonwealth Trust Company, and that it would act as trustee, fulfilling all stipulations of the original trust indenture.

Valiantly the project's sales force "ran around and bought notes from those who wanted their money back." Of course, many subscribers were scattered all over the nation and couldn't be reached. One million dollars was salvaged. With this money, 3200 acres of the property, which is now Miraleste and the City of Palos Verdes Estates, were purchased.

Managers for the revived Palos Verdes Project, now a real estate trust financed by some 4000 investors, were Jay Lawyer of the Vanderlip syndicate, J.H. Coverly, formerly with the Title Insurance Company, and E.G. Lewis. Mr. Lewis resigned within two months, and the Commonwealth Trust Company merged into the Bank of America, Los Angeles, on September 28, 1923.

Many of the men, who from the beginning had been part of the great dream for development of Los Palos Verdes, continued to serve in this phase of the undertaking. Notable among them were Frederick Law Olmsted, Charles H. Cheney and Myron Hunt. To insure that the dream would not be despoiled, they took immediate steps to preserve the unique beauty of the land.

Protective restrictions were drawn up, an Art Jury was established, and a community association composed of property owners was incorporated under the name Palos Verdes Homes Association. Legal power was vested in the Homes Association and the Art Jury to enforce the restrictions, as they were made part of the deed to every parcel of land in Palos Verdes Estates and Miraleste.

Life of the Restrictions was to extend for thirty-seven years, with automatic extension provided for successive twenty-year periods unless then changed by two-thirds of the property owners. They were extremely detailed, implementing the master plan drawn by Charles H. Cheney for development of the entire acreage.

Half of Palos Verdes Estates was reserved for parklands and public rights of way. Ninety per cent of all lots were restricted to one-family houses. The four principal communities of Malaga Cove, Lunada Bay, Valmonte, and Miraleste were allowed, "as a matter of convenience, reasonably small business centers." Each such center was to be built around a plaza, with all buildings arcaded on the ground floors. Types of architecture were specified and the smallest details of exterior design regulated. For example, on the hillside areas the roof pitch was limited and red tile required to enhance the loveliness of the vistas sweeping down to the sea.

Now a tremendous real estate campaign was launched. Every effort was made to sell lots. On Sunday afternoons there were programs of music, Spanish dancing, stunt flying, aquaplaning and yacht racing. Crowds assembled on the land where the Malaga Cove School now stands. One Sunday, 800 automobile parties came in response to the forceful advertising program. Free coffee and lunch were provided, and there was "even a Kiddies' Tent at Palos Verdes, on these important afternoons, with playground teachers, physicians and free toys." (W.W. Robinson)

High on a hill, a charming inn was built by the managers of the Project. Significantly it was named La Venta, the primary meaning of the word *venta* being sale. It was used as a place to bring prominent prospective buyers. There they were entertained and intoxicated with the breathtakingly beautiful setting.

Meanwhile hundreds of thousands of trees and shrubs were planted. The Olmsted Brothers were leaders in the field of landscape architecture; among their many achievements was the design of Central Park in New York. Mr. Olmsted transformed the northern entrance to the Estates into an all-year garden of radiant bloom, and the slopes back of Malaga Cove into 55 acres of park, planted in masses of eucalyptus, pine, and cypress. Concerned not only for the beauty of public parklands but also for the individual homesites, he established a nursery at Lunada Bay where residents could obtain plants at cost and he gave neighborly advice on landscaping.

Early in 1924, homes began to appear, dotted around on the open fields of grain. The real estate promotion had paid off. Many people had purchased lots, some for homebuilding, others for speculation. Schemes were devised by the Project to encourage people to build. One hundred dollars in gold was offered for the first house started, and fifty for the second.

Many of these residences were small, about a thousand square feet;

others were palatial, like the Olmsted home near the northwest corner of the Estates. But before long, half a million dollars worth of building permits were issued in the space of a year. And each house, large or small, was individually designed to fit attractively into its surroundings.

Palos Verdes was "way out in the country." The people who came to live there valued the isolation and untamed beauty of the Peninsula. One early resident expressed the feeling of those first families as, "all the hills belonged to us." There were many inconveniences but they were more than compensated for by the warm friendly atmosphere of the community. "Everyone counted. Everyone was needed and wanted."

Great emphasis was placed upon family gatherings. Community Thanksgiving and Christmas celebrations were held in the residents' homes. One of the most delightful of these was the annual ceremony of Las Posadas, started in 1924.

A procession bearing lighted candles, led by two children dressed as Mary and Joseph, walked single file down the long, dark, winding road from the Plaza to the Olmsted residence. There after "Mary and Joseph" had knocked symbolically at each of three doors, the whole group entered the long candlelit living room and listened to the reading of the Nativity story. This ceremony was followed by carole singing, refreshments, and the breaking of the huge piñata hung from the ceiling in the center of the room.

Many of the original settlers were members of the Project staff, who brought with them a strong New England influence. Out of this came another charming community custom, the annual Colonial Ball, celebrating Washington's birthday. Held in the Malaga Cove School auditorium, decorated for the occasion with a hundred potted shrubs, it was a stunning affair.

For weeks the women of the community prepared for the event. Silks and satins were hand-sewn into beautiful costumes for everyone, including the children. On the evening of the ball, a gay throng, attired in bouffant skirts and knee breeches, with white periwigs and powdered hair, assembled in the softly flickering candlelight. A grand march was executed, followed by the children's minuet. Then the group spent the evening dancing the waltz, two-step, and Virginia reel.

While this closely knit social life was evolving, significant strides were taking place in other areas of community development. On a sunny Sunday afternoon in September, 1925, a celebration was held in the Plaza to dedicate the first business building. Now colloquially referred to as "the drugstore building," the Gardner Building was in the Spanish

Renaissance style, with roof composed of handmade Mexican tile. Prominent city and county officials gathered for the ceremony, and Charles Cheney proudly announced, "Palos Verdes today has become a full-fledged community."

Among the requisites of a community are roads, and these were a real test for the Project planners. They had to design them to fit the natural contours of the land, minimizing ugly cuts and fills. Miles of curving streets were the result. The biggest challenge came in building a highway along the Peninsula's rugged shoreline.

Near Bluff Cove a formidable ridge extended seaward from the heights of Montemalaga. Here the old ranch road toiled up an 18 per cent grade. On October 17, 1923, a crowd of over 20,000 people came to watch the discharge of sixty tons of blasting powder. The "Douglas Cut" formed a new beach line and reduced the elevation of the final grade from 420 to 320 feet.

To construct one hundred feet of road, at this point, required the moving of 30,000 cubic yards of material and cost $90,000. On July 31, 1926, the scenic shore road was completed. Led by four county motorcycle officers, a caravan of 300 automobiles traversed the twenty-mile route from Ninth Street in San Pedro, through Miraleste, and over what are today Palos Verdes Drive South and Palos Verdes Drive West to the Plaza.

By 1930, the major portion of the Palos Verdes Project was completed. Roads had been constructed and the first school built. The Plaza boasted a second business building as well as the spectacular Fountain of Neptune, and the Palos Verdes Library and Art Gallery had opened its doors. Over a period of time, as plans for the Project were realized, its managers had been transferring affairs of government to the Palos Verdes Homes Association. In 1931 this organization assumed complete control.

While the Palos Verdes Project was progressing, Frank Vanderlip had been developing his plan for a beautiful country estate at Portuguese Bend. It was to center around an Italian villa, high on a hill overlooking the sea. Architectural plans were drawn, patterning the mansion after the ancient Roman Villa Papa Julio, and a detailed plaster model was constructed by the noted French landscape designer Jacques Greber. During the 1920s, thousands of trees and shrubs were planted on the estate, and the utilitarian portion of the villa complex was completed. This was a replica of a Tuscany farmhouse of the Renaissance period, termed the "Farmstead," with servants' quarters, stables, and garages surrounding an open courtyard.

In 1924, Mr. Vanderlip built the "Villetta," which he intended as a guesthouse, and a long stately staircase led from it to where the villa was to be. Back of the "Villetta" a flight of 268 stone steps soared to a spectacular lookout point where a white marble temple was erected. Seeds for the cypress trees, which lined both staircases, were collected in the Bogoli gardens in Rome by members of the Vanderlip family.

Although their home base was near Scarborough, New York, Frank and Narcissa Vanderlip, and their six children, spent a great deal of time at Portuguese Bend. It was here that Mr. Vanderlip indulged some of his most cherished hobbies. Among these was his fabulous collection of birds, four acres of bird runs, and over five hundred varieties of birds. In later years, all but the peacocks were given to the Wrigley family and became the nucleus of the famed "Bird Farm" on Catalina Island.

During the 1920s, two other families built homes at Portuguese Bend. In 1926 Harry Benedict, friend and business associate of Mr. Vanderlip, built the elegant Villa Francesca, named after his wife, Frances; and Edward Harden, whose wife was Mrs. Vanderlip's sister, built the lodge at Portuguese Bend. There were five buildings, including the original "Cottage," along a horseshoe-shaped road that had two entrances on what is now Palos Verdes Drive South.

Mr. Vanderlip also dreamed of building a hillside town in the vicinity of Point Vicente and the present-day Marineland. Plaster models were constructed for an artisan village, comprising three-story stucco homes with workshops on the lower level, as well as several community buildings. All of the architecture was designed to recreate the ambiance of an Italian hill-town.

Unfortunately, the depression stymied the realization of Mr. Vanderlip's dreams. Neither the village nor the villa, which was to crown his great estate, was destined to materialize. However, the carefully crafted plaster models have been preserved and are now the property of the Rancho de los Palos Verdes Historical Society.

At the time the depression struck, there were also ambitious plans for all of the Palos Verdes Peninsula. A layout for the entire 16,000 acres had been prepared by the Olmsted Brothers. It included residential and business districts, schools, parks, golf courses, and even an airport.

Drawings for the Lunada Bay Plaza portray an old Spanish town, with lantern towers, winding stairways and a fountain. A palatial yacht club was to be built near Bluff Cove. A yacht harbor big enough to provide stillwater mooring for 400 craft and a breakwater to enclose some 66 acres of water were included in the plans.

In 1930 national magazines were carrying rhapsodical tributes to Palos Verdes. Louis Bromfield paid homage in *Vogue*—"in Palos Verdes . . . one has the impression of entering a paradise designed by the Spanish for the anointed of Heaven." By 1931, there was serious trouble in paradise.

The bottom fell out of real estate, the Palos Verdes Homes Association was able to collect only 20 per cent of the maintenance assessments levied on property owners, and county taxes on the Palos Verdes parklands were allowed to go delinquent. For the next seven years, slowly and inexorably, the situation worsened.

At the time, more than half of the land in Palos Verdes Estates was still in the hands of a real estate firm called Palos Verdes Estates, Inc., which had replaced the Project sales organization. Its manager, Oscar Willett, came to Palos Verdes as trustee appointed by the Federal Court for the creditors of E.G. Lewis; that is, holders of nonconvertible subscription notes still unredeemed. His solution for the plight of Palos Verdes was a forceful sales promotion. For this he needed a newspaper, and he was willing to support it with real estate advertising. He interested John Knezevich in his plan and in 1937 the Palos Verdes *News* came into being.

The sales campaign was a success. Ninety-one lots, worth over $100,000 were sold in ten days and by the end of the year over half a million dollars in building permits were issued. But the financial condition of Palos Verdes Estates was not cured. In May, 1938, the Homes Association owed over $33,000 to Los Angeles County in back taxes. The day of reckoning was at hand.

A representative of the County Auditor's office stated flatly that the only way the delinquent taxes could be canceled was for the Homes Association to turn the parklands over to the County. An alternate solution was that a large portion of Lunada Bay, specifically the areas of Resort Point and Bluff Cove, be deeded to the County to be used as public parks, picnic grounds, and beaches. Such a transaction would cancel the unpaid taxes of both the Homes Association and Palos Verdes Estates, Inc., as the real estate firm owned part of this land and was tax delinquent in the amount of $260,000.

Residents rose up in rebellion. The prospects of public parks represented a threat to the beloved community. The cry was that the "deal" would "ruin" Palos Verdes. But there were some voices raised in support of the plan. Charles Cheney felt that it was better to preserve the parklands at any cost. Oscar Willett saw public parks as a tourist attraction that would aid in the sale of real estate. In the midst of the hue and cry, the county withdrew its offer to purchase the Lunada Bay property.

The Homes Association appointed two committees in succession to come up with an acceptable solution. The second committee proposed that Palos Verdes be incorporated into a city, thus acquiring permanent title to its parklands. The president of the Homes Association proposed the formation of a park and recreation district to which the parklands could be deeded. Once again the battle lines were drawn.

The proponents of the incorporation feared the loss of the parklands. The opponents feared the lowering of restrictions and ''double taxation.'' The ensuing campaign was long and bitter. The once closely knit community split into hostile camps. Finally in September, 1939, a sufficient number of signatures was obtained to petition the County Board of Supervisors for an election. On December 9th the people of Palos Verdes voted themselves a city, by the narrow margin of seven votes.

In the meantime, the Homes Association had been working to straighten out its financial situation. A settlement was made with Palos Verdes Estates, Inc. for the better then $50,000 which the land corporation owed in delinquent assessments. Then suits were filed to collect approximately $17,000 owed to the Association by individual property owners. Legal action also was taken to make it possible for the Association to assess improvements as well as land. As a result, its income was almost doubled.

Considerable friction had developed between the Homes Association and Palos Verdes Estates, Inc. Many people felt that the realtors, while primarily concerned with interests of the noteholders, were dominating the affairs of the community. Tension was relieved when all remaining property owned by the corporation was liquidated at a huge public auction, held in the Plaza in July, 1939. Now Palos Verdes Estates belonged to its people and could make a fresh start in its new status of city of the sixth class.

But the great plan for development of the Peninsula as a whole never was revived. The Depression resulted in fragmentation, although Frank A. Vanderlip did what he could to preserve the lovely terraced land. In November, 1925, he had formed the Palos Verdes Corporation to handle the remaining acreage, and more than ten years later, in 1936, the first subdivision was opened.

This was the area which became the City of Rolling Hills, a community so unique that the only other development with which it can be compared is Tuxedo Park in New York. Completely enclosed by white split-rail fencing, it is characterized by densely wooded, rolling hills, large country estates and miles of riding trails. From the very beginning a community association established and enforced rigid restrictions. And in January, 1957, residents voted to incorporate in order to preserve the rural atmosphere they prized.

With the death of Frank A. Vanderlip in 1937, control of the Palos Verdes Corporation went to his son, Frank Jr., who served as President until he was succeeded by Harry Benedict, in 1943. During most of this period Portuguese Bend remained open country, noted for its rugged beauty and uninhabited except for visits from the three families who had built there in the 1920s. It became a favorite spot for private picnic parties, brought by launch from San Pedro and Redondo, and for a short time there was a small seaside cafe on the beach below the bluffs.

In 1945, the late Mr. Vanderlip's second son, Kelvin, became President of the Palos Verdes Corporation. He shared many of the ideals and concepts that had motivated his father. With his charming wife, Elin, he took up residence at the "Villetta" and resumed development of the area. A complex of carefully planned streets was constructed off the horseshoe-shaped road that served the Vanderlip estate, and 1100 acres of land were opened for homes. A community association was formed to insure the quality of the development, and the fashionable Portuguese Bend Club became the nucleus of the new community.

Then in October, 1950, Frank A. Vanderlip, Jr. was re-elected President of the Palos Verdes Corporation, and in July, 1953, the event occurred which was to have a more far-reaching effect on the future of the Peninsula than any other single happening in its history. Since 1944, a three-hundred-acre tract of land on the north side of the Peninsula had been leased to the Great Lakes Carbon Corporation for the mining of diatomaceous earth. Though this tract's diatomite reserves were almost exhausted, another rich deposit was known to exist in a 165-acre tract near the crest of the Palos Verdes Hills. For more than two years, officials of Great Lakes Carbon had been endeavoring to purchase this land without success. Then Frank Vanderlip agreed to sell, provided the corporation bought all the stock of the Palos Verdes Corporation.

Nine million dollars was the purchase price for the 7000 acres, all that was left of the 16,000 acres bought from Mr. Bixby with the exception of about 500 acres retained by the Vanderlip family. Thus, upon consummation of the deal, the Great Lakes Carbon Corporation assumed ownership of practically all of the still-undeveloped portion of the

Peninsula. Not long after, plans for the mining operation were discarded. Instead, a group of well-known architects and engineers was engaged to develop "the most outstanding planned community in the United States." Once again developers came with a master plan. This time they had the power to bring their plans to fruition.

Much of the original goal was achieved, although many people lament the vast changes that have taken place. It is true that development has left scars. But time has altered only the surface of the terraced land. Still the proud headland thrusts out to sea, and its incomparable vistas enthrall the hearts and minds of man. Millions of years in the making, the shape of beauty stands, separated by its towering ridge from the hectic, hurly-burly of modern city life. For tens of thousands of families, it has been the promise of paradise fulfilled.

SEPÚLVEDA FAMILY GENEALOGY

Francisco Xavier Sepúlveda ——┬—— María Candelaría de Redondo

JUAN JOSÉ SEPÚLVEDA
Married Tomasa Gutiérrez — 1786

JOSÉ DOLORES SEPÚLVEDA
1793 - 1824
Married María Ygnacia Avíla — 1813

1 JUAN CAPISTRANO
1814 - 1896
Married Felipa Alanis — 1836
Married Susana Ruiz — 1868

2 JOSÉ LORETO
1815 - 1881
Married Cesaria Pantoja — 1835
Married Teodocia Gonzalez — 1875

3 YGNACIO RAFAEL
1819-1847

4 JOSÉ DIEGO
1820 - 1869
Married María Francisca Elizalde — 1843

5 MARÍA TERESA
1823 - 1840
Married Nathaniel Pryor - 1838

Bibliography

Balls, Edward K. *Early Uses of California Plants.* Berkeley: University of California Press, 1962.

Bancroft, Hubert Howe, *History of California,* Volumes I, II, III. San Francisco: The History Company, 1886–1890.

———, *California Pastoral, 1769–1848.* San Francisco: The History Company, 1888.

Bartlett, Lanier, *Los Angeles in 7 days, including Southern California.* New York: Robert M. McBride & Co., 1932.

Bauer, Helen, *California Indian Days.* Garden City, N.Y.: Doubleday, 1963.

Bell, Horace, *Reminiscences of a Ranger.* Santa Barbara, California: Wallace Hebberd, 1927.

Bolton, Herbert Eugene, *Spanish Explorations in the Southwest.* New York: Scribner, 1916.

Cleland, Robert Glass, *From Wilderness to Empire, a History of California.* New York: Alfred Knopf, 1962.

———, *Cattle on a Thousand Hills, Southern California, 1850–1880.*

San Marino, California: The Huntington Library, 1951.

Dana, Richard Henry, *Two Years Before the Mast.* Boston: Houghton, Mifflin & Co., 1911.

Gillingham, Robert Cameron, *The Rancho San Pedro.* Los Angeles: The Dominguez Estate Company, 1961.

Guinn, J.M., *Historical and Biographical Record of Los Angeles and Vicinity.* Chicago: The Chapman Publishing Co., 1901.

Johnston, Bernice Eastman, *California's Gabrielino Indians.* Los Angeles: The Southwest Museum, 1962.

Kelsey, Harry, *Juan Rodríguez Cabrillo.* San Marino, California: The Huntington Library, 1986.

Krythe, Maymie, *Port Admiral: Phineas Banning.* San Francisco: The California Historical Society, 1957.

Lord, Eliot, *Comstock Mining and Miners,* Berkeley, California: Howell-North, 1959.

Ludwig, Ella A., *A History of the Harbor District of Los Angeles.* California: Historic Record Company, Inc., n.d.

McWilliams, Carey, *Southern California Country: An Island on the Land.* New York: Duell, Sloan & Pearce, 1946.

Matson, Clarence, *Building a World Gateway.* Los Angeles: Pacific Era Publishers, 1945.

Nadeau, Remi, *Los Angeles from Mission to Modern City.* New York: Longmans, Green & Co., 1960.

Newmark, Harris, *Sixty Years in Southern California, 1853–1913.* Boston: Riverside Press, 1930.

Padilla, Victoria, *Southern California Gardens.* Berkeley: University of California Press, 1961.

Pourade, Richard F., *History of San Diego—The Explorers,* Volume I. San Diego: Union-Tribune Publishing Co., 1960.

———, *History of San Diego—The Time of the Bells,* Volume II. San Diego: Union-Tribune Publishing Co., 1961.

Reiter, Martin, *The Palos Verdes Peninsula, A Geologic Guide and More.* Dubuque, Iowa: Kendall/Hunt Publishing Company, 1984.

Robinson, Alfred, *Life in California.* Oakland, California: Biobooks, 1947.

Robinson, W.W., *Los Angeles from the Days of the Pueblo.* San Francisco: California Historical Society, 1959.

————, *Ranchos Become Cities.* Pasadena, California: San Pasqual Press, 1939.

Scammon, Charles M., *The Marine Animals of the North Western Coast of North America, described and illustrated: Together with an account of the American Whale Fishery.* San Francisco, California: John H. Carmany and Company, 1874.

Smith, Sarah Bixby, *Adobe Days.* Los Angeles: Jake Zeitlin, 1931.

Temple, Thomas Workman, Jr., *Memoirs of José Francisco Palomares.* Los Angeles: Glen Dawson, 1955.

Thompson and West, *History of Los Angeles County.* Berkeley: Howell-North, 1959.

Tompkins, Walker, *Santa Barbara's Royal Rancho,* Berkeley, California: Howell-North, 1960.

Wilbur, Marguerite E., editor, *Vancouver in California.* Los Angeles: Glen Dawson, 1954.

Willard, Charles Dwight, *The Free Harbor Contest.* Los Angeles: Kingsley-Barnes & Neuner, 1899.

PAMPHLETS AND PERIODICALS

Ainsworth, Ed, *Enchanted Pueblo.* Los Angeles: Bank of America, 1959.

Bixby Records Collection. Palos Verdes Library and Art Gallery.

Bliss, Carey, *The Free Harbor Contest or Citizen Versus Railroad.* San Francisco: Book Club of California, 1954.

The Commonwealth. Atascadero, California: (no date or publisher) 1922.

Kiessling, Edmund, *A Trip to Palos Verdes Hills.* San Francisco: Mineral Information Service, Division of Mines and Geology, State of California, Vol. XVI, Number 11, 1963.

Los Angeles Board of Harbor Commissioners. *Annual Report, 1964.*

————, "Let's Tour the Harbor," 1964.

————, "Points of Interest in the Greater Los Angeles Area"

McQuat, H.W., *Case History of Los Angeles Harbor.* Long Beach, California: Institute on Coastal Engineering, 1950.

Palmer, Conner, *The Romance of the Ranchos*. Los Angeles: Title In-Insurance & Trust Co., 1941.

Palos Verdes *Bulletin*. Published by the Palos Verdes Homes Association, Nov., 1923–October, 1931.

Palos Verdes Estates *Protective Restrictions*. Compiled by Olmsted Brothers and C.H. Cheney, no date or publisher given.

Palos Verdes *Review*. The Palos Verdes Story, by Delane Morgan, September, 1963–December, 1964.

Railway and Locomotive Historical Society. Bulletin No. 97, October, 1957.

Robinson, W.W., *San Pedro and Wilmington: A Calendar of Events in the Making of Two Cities and the Los Angeles Harbor*. Los Angeles: Title Guarantee & Trust Co., 1937.

———, *Panorama: a Picture History of Southern California*. Los Angeles: Title Insurance & Trust Co., 1953.

———, *Southern California Real Estate Boom of the Twenties*. Los Angeles: *Historical Society of Southern California Quarterly*, March, 1942.

Stimson, Marshall, "A Short History of Los Angeles Harbor." Los Angeles: *Historical Society of Southern California Quarterly*, March, 1945.

Walker, Edwin Francis, *Five Prehistoric Archeological Sites in Los Angeles County*. Los Angeles: Southwest Museum, 1951.

NEWSPAPERS

Boston *Evening Transcript*, July 18, 1914.

Palos Verdes *News*, 1937–1965.

San Pedro *News Pilot Anniversary Edition*, August 14, 1959. "Outline History of the Harbor Area," by Anna Marie & Everett Gordon Hager.

MANUSCRIPTS

Grounds, Marr Roy, *The Farmstead*. University of California, Berkeley, 1959.

Sten, Pod, *The Story of San Pedro Harbor: Ships and Rails.* (Approximate date: 1930–1933, never submitted).

Thacker, Mary Eva, *A History of Los Palos Verdes Rancho, 1542–1923,* University of California, Berkeley, May 1, 1923.

Index

(* denotes illustration or map)